The Life of Christ

Zondervan Quick-Reference Library

**ZONDERVAN
QUICK
REFERENCE
LIBRARY**

The Life
of Christ

John H.
Sailhamer

ZondervanPublishingHouse

Grand Rapids, Michigan

A Division of HarperCollinsPublishers

The Life of Christ
Copyright © 1998 by John H. Sailhamer

Requests for information should be addressed to:

■ ZondervanPublishingHouse
Grand Rapids, Michigan 49530

Library of Congress Cataloging-in-Publication Data

Sailhamer, John.
    The life of Christ / John H. Sailhamer.
        p.   cm. — (Zondervan quick-reference library)
    ISBN: 0-310-20392-9 (softcover)
    1. Jesus Christ—Biography. I. Title. II. Series.
BT301.2.S134 1998
232.6'01-dc 21   97-46008
                                          CIP

Interior design by Sue Vandenberg Koppenol

Printed in the United States of America

98 99 00 01 02 03 04 /❖ DC/ 10 9 8 7 6 5 4 3 2 1

Contents

Abbreviations
of the Books of the Bible

Genesis	Gen.	Nahum	Nah.
Exodus	Ex.	Habakkuk	Hab.
Leviticus	Lev.	Zephaniah	Zeph.
Numbers	Num.	Haggai	Hag.
Deuteronomy	Deut.	Zechariah	Zech.
Joshua	Josh.	Malachi	Mal.
Judges	Judg.	Matthew	Matt.
Ruth	Ruth	Mark	Mark
1 Samuel	1 Sam.	Luke	Luke
2 Samuel	2 Sam.	John	John
1 Kings	1 Kings	Acts	Acts
2 Kings	2 Kings	Romans	Rom.
1 Chronicles	1 Chron.	1 Corinthians	1 Cor.
2 Chronicles	2 Chron.	2 Corinthians	2 Cor.
Ezra	Ezra	Galatians	Gal.
Nehemiah	Neh.	Ephesians	Eph.
Esther	Est.	Philippians	Phil.
Job	Job	Colossians	Col.
Psalms	Ps(s).	1 Thessalonians	1 Thess.
Proverbs	Prov.	2 Thessalonians	2 Thess.
Ecclesiastes	Eccl.	1 Timothy	1 Tim.
Song of Songs	Song	2 Timothy	2 Tim.
Isaiah	Isa.	Titus	Titus
Jeremiah	Jer.	Philemon	Philem.
Lamentations	Lam.	Hebrews	Heb.
Ezekiel	Ezek.	James	James
Daniel	Dan.	1 Peter	1 Peter
Hosea	Hos.	2 Peter	2 Peter
Joel	Joel	1 John	1 John
Amos	Amos	2 John	2 John
Obadiah	Obad.	3 John	3 John
Jonah	Jonah	Jude	Jude
Micah	Mic.	Revelation	Rev.

The Gospels

What is the *Zondervan Quick-Reference Library: Life of Christ?*

The *Zondervan Quick-Reference Library: Life of Christ* is a new and unique reference tool. Simply put, it is a complete and comprehensive account of the life of Jesus Christ. Because we get much of our information in daily life quickly and efficiently, we are becoming increasingly accustomed to having knowledge about the Bible also given to us in the same way. There is a legitimate need for a more efficient way to gain information about the Bible—if only as a starting point for more in-depth and reflective understanding. Once we get a sense of what a subject such as the life of Christ is about, the details begin to make more sense. A regular use of this *Life of Christ* book should lead to a more knowledgeable study of God's Word. This book is a convenient starting point for gaining a more comprehensive understanding of the Scriptures. It has two distinct features: (1) a series of introductory pages, intended to bring the reader up to speed on the study of the Gospels and the life of Christ; (2) a historical and chronological account of the events in the life of Christ.

A word is needed about the kind of historical account of the life of Christ offered in this book. Many accounts of his life have been written. In important ways, this one is unique. If you look closely at the accounts of Christ's life currently available, most retell the story from two perspectives: (1) the accounts given in the four Gospels in the New Testament, and (2) historical and archaeological sources from New Testament times. In such accounts, the material taken from the Gospels is usually fit into the broader scheme of first-century Roman and Palestinian history. The "big picture," then, is taken from extrabiblical history and the life of Christ is fit into that picture. Moreover, many historical details of first-century Palestine are added to "fill-out" the picture of Christ.

We have chosen not to take that approach. Rather, we have limited ourselves almost entirely to the account of Christ's life as seen within the four Gospels. Naturally some reference is made to persons and locations known to us from history, but the story itself comes from the biblical text. By viewing the events of Christ's life internally from the four perspectives of the Gospels, we attempt to "see the whole" of his life as the biblical authors themselves present it. There are advantages, of course, to both approaches, but we feel a need for the type of account of Christ's life given in this book.

Gospel in the New Testament

Our knowledge of the life of Christ comes almost entirely from the pages of the four Gospels—Matthew, Mark, Luke, and John. These are literary works, whose intent is to give a historical portrait of the man Jesus. Each Gospel has its own point of view and presents the life of Christ from that perspective.

What kind of literary texts are these Gospels? We must know how to answer that question to fully appreciate the picture of Jesus that each Gospel gives. We begin our look at the life of Jesus with a brief description of the sources we will use.

The general meaning of the Greek term for *gospel* (*euangelion*) is "good news." In the New Testament this term means specifically "the message of salvation"—the message of Christ's work in his life, death, and resurrection. First Corinthians 15:3–5 contains an early summary: "that Christ died for our sins according to the Scriptures, that he was buried, that he was raised on the third day according to the Scriptures, and that he appeared to [various of his followers]."

As this early statement shows, the gospel focused on Jesus' deeds rather than on his teachings. This message served as the basis of the preaching of the early church; thus, in New Testament usage, *gospel* applies mainly to the preached message about Jesus Christ. Those who preached the gospel were known as the evangelists (cf. Acts 21:8; Eph. 4:11; 2 Tim. 4:5).

There is at least one example in the New Testament, however, where the written account of the life of Christ is itself called a "gospel"—Mark 1:1, "the beginning of the gospel about Jesus Christ." Beyond this example, within the written texts themselves are helpful clues as to how these Gospels were originally conceived of by their authors. In John 20:30, for example, the author refers to his Gospel as "this book" or "this scroll." According to Luke 1:1 the earliest written accounts of Jesus' life were called simply "accounts" or "narratives." By the beginning of the second century, *gospel* as used in Mark seems to have become a general title for the written story about Jesus Christ (Didache 15:3–4; 2 Clement 8:5).

The Genre "Gospel"

For the most part, the written documents we call Gospels should be understood as simple narrative texts of the life, death, and resurrection of Jesus. Their purpose was to link the message of the gospel to the details of Jesus' life and teaching, and their goal was the explication and clarification of the message of the cross. Mark alone entitles his work a "gospel." We need to ask what the "genre" of this form of writing is.

It is generally agreed that the New Testament Gospel narratives do not correspond to any literary form known in the literature of the ancient world. The reason for this, no doubt, lies in the fact that behind these Gospels stands a unique event—the incarnation, death, and resurrection of Jesus, the Lord. A unique event called for a unique genre of literature.

A comparison with literary forms of the ancient world reveals several unique features of the Gospels. They do not, for example, conform to the normal form of the ancient historical writings such as biographies or memoirs. They do not show an interest in developing the personality of Jesus, his personal and family background, or his education and his human character. Moreover, they do not contain references to the thoughts and opinions of their authors—in fact, they do not even contain an indication of who their authors were.

In other words, the form of the Gospels appears to be determined by their unique purpose—to bring together the words and deeds of the historical Jesus in a way that demonstrates the significance of his life, death, and resurrection.

The Gospels and the Historical Jesus

Do the Gospels give us a true historical picture of the life of Christ? Does the picture they give of Christ's life conform to whatever facts we might arrive at outside the Gospels themselves? Can we know the "historical Jesus" by reading the Gospels? Such questions lie at the heart of the study of the life of Christ. Obviously, if we want to learn about the life of Christ, we need to know whether our sources are reliable witnesses to the facts.

There are several good reasons for concluding that the Gospels do, in fact, present a historically reliable picture of Jesus. First of all, history and the writing of history was well known in the ancient world. The historical books of the Old Testament are a prime example of the concern of ancient historians to present past events in a logical and orderly fashion. Greek historians such as Herodotus (ca. 490–425 B.C.), Thucydides (ca. 460–399 B.C.), and Polybius (ca. 200–118 B.C.) established a firm foundation for later Jewish historians, such as the authors of the books of Maccabees and Josephus, to build on and emulate.

The Gospel writers give every indication that they followed the examples of earlier historians in their accounts of the life of Jesus. Luke tells his readers specifically how he arrived at his sources for writing about Jesus (Luke 1:1–4). All the Gospel writers tie their accounts of the life of Jesus into larger historical events. John tells us the name of the high priest, Caiaphas, at the time of Jesus. Luke begins his account of John the Baptist with the note, "In the fifteenth year of the reign of Tiberius Caesar—when Pontius Pilate was governor of Judea, Herod tetrarch of Galilee, his brother Philip tetrarch of Iturea and Traconitis, and Lysanias tetrarch of Abilene . . ." (Luke 3:1). The detailed accounts of everyday life in first-century Palestine, found throughout the Gospels, are today highly regarded as perhaps the best historical sources for that period.

Furthermore, many early manuscript copies of the Gospels still exist today. The life of Christ is certainly the most documented event of the ancient world.

The Synoptic Problem I

The first three Gospels, Matthew, Mark, and Luke, give evidence of a close literary relationship as well as of a marked independence of each of them. The attempt to explain these two facets is the concern of what has come to be known as "The Synoptic Problem."

A clear similarity exists among Matthew, Mark, and Luke in the general structure of the narrative. All three follow the same basic sequence of events: They begin with the baptism of Jesus and his temptation in the desert; then follows the public ministry of Jesus in Galilee, his last journey to Jerusalem, and his trial, crucifixion, and resurrection. These three Gospels devote much of their attention to the details of the last week before Christ's death. Furthermore, all three appear to have the same basic purpose—to recount the deeds and words of Jesus. Finally, each Gospel is composed of small, self-contained units. Some (such as the parable of the sower) are found in all three Gospels, while others are found in only one or two of them.

The similarity among the three Gospels can also be seen in many details, such as similar vocabulary and style. To get a sense of this one need only compare the account of Jesus' healing of a leper (Matt. 8:1–4; Mark 1:40–45; Luke 5:12–16) or his feeding of the five thousand (Matt. 14:19; Mark 6:41; Luke 9:16). It is not uncommon to find that when all three Gospels recount the same story, two will be similar while the third may show a difference in vocabulary (see, e.g., Matt. 20:24–28; Mark 10:41–45; Luke 22:24–27).

Such similarities stand in contrast to other features that suggest a marked independence in the composition of each of the first three Gospels. The account of Jesus' birth in Matthew and Luke, for example, show little or no signs of a close relationship. Matthew writes about the birth of Jesus from the viewpoint of Joseph, while Luke tells of the same event from that of his mother, Mary. Matthew mentions the visit of the Magi and the flight to Egypt, but these events are not found in Luke. Matthew gives an account of the Sermon on the Mount but Mark omits it.

The Synoptic Problem II

How are these characteristics of the first three Gospels to be explained? They suggest that there is, indeed, a real literary dependence of the Gospels on each other. The authors of one or more of the Gospels appear to have borrowed material from the others, but they also added material of their own. Luke states as much at the beginning of his account (Luke 1:1–4).

Moreover, it appears that the first three Gospels were not all written at the same time. One of them, probably Mark, was written before the other two and served as the basis for them. But the acceptance of the priority of Mark raises another question: How do we explain those places in Matthew and Luke where similar material is found but where Mark has nothing that parallels it? In other words, Matthew and Luke not only appeared to have used Mark, but they also must have used common material not found in Mark.

This common material is today often called "Q" (named for the German word for "source," that is, *Quelle*). The acceptance of the priority of Mark also implies the acceptance of at least two more sources—M and L, that is, material found only in Matthew (M) or Luke (L).

On the basis of these observations, the most widely held view today is that Mark's Gospel was written first and that both Matthew and Luke used it and other sources to complete their works. This explanation adequately explains the similarities and differences among the three Gospels. Moreover, it accords well with the situation known from Luke's prologue (Luke 1:1–4), the one clear statement on sources that we have from the texts themselves. Evidence from studies in oral tradition suggest that a "document" such as Q could have been in existence at an early stage.

The Synoptic Problem III

We know from the New Testament itself that certain "sayings" of Jesus did circulate in Asia Minor before A.D. 57, the time of Paul's farewell address at Miletus (Acts 20:35). Here Paul admonished the elders of Ephesus to remember "the words the Lord Jesus himself said: 'It is more blessed to give than to receive.'" Since this saying of Jesus is not found in the Gospels, there was apparently some means of preserving the sayings of Jesus. The apostle Paul himself also appears to have had access to a collection of the sayings of Jesus and assumes that his readers in Corinth were familiar with them. Note 1 Corinthians 7:10, where Paul refers to the Lord's teaching on marriage, which is later recorded in Mark (Mark 10:6–9; cf. Matt. 19:8–10).

The process of using earlier documents to write Scripture was not uncommon. The book of Chronicles, for example, used and even cited other sources (1 Chron. 29:29). In Ezra 6:2, the biblical writer clearly indicates his use of a source from the actual Aramaic memorandum of the records of the Persian empire.

There are, of course, weaknesses to the theory that Mark was the first Gospel. How do we explain, for example, those places in Matthew and Luke where they are similar but Mark has something different (cf. Mark 3:23 with Matt. 12:25; Luke 11:17)? Did Matthew and Luke sometimes share another source than Mark? Did Luke use Matthew in such cases? If so, there would be no reason to suppose Luke ever used Mark.

And what about "Q"? There is no direct historical evidence for it. True, this "document" could have been a kind of oral tradition, thus eliminating the need of a written copy of Q. There is still much we do not know about the relationship among the Synoptic Gospels. Fortunately, in the last analysis, an understanding of each Gospel is not dependent on our solving the Synoptic problem. From the Gospels themselves it is clear that each is an independent literary work that can be understood by reading it. Each one has its own particular purpose and audience in mind.

The World of Jesus

Historical Geography of Palestine I

The last events recorded in the Old Testament Scriptures occurred during the heyday of the Persian empire. During this period the once vast kingdom of David was reduced to a small province. Instead of a royal scion from the house of David, an obscure governor ruled God's people. The last we hear of the internal events of the life of this people in the Bible are the records of Ezra and Nehemiah (445 B.C.). The earliest Jewish histories after this time begin from the time of the Maccabean revolt in the mid–second century B.C. Between these two dates, little is known of the internal affairs of the Jewish people in Palestine.

Some knowledge of this period can be gained from the Elephantine Papyri, Jewish Aramaic documents discovered in Egypt in 1906–1908. These documents consist mostly of letters written by Jewish soldiers in Egypt to a governor of Judah named Bagoas and to other officials, from 495–399 B.C. Apart from these letters, archaeological excavations have produced coins and artifacts that demonstrate a thriving political and social life during this time.

On the world scene, the central event of this period was the decline and fall of the Persian empire by the middle of the fourth century. The last Persian king, Darius III (335–330 B.C.), faced rebellion from within his own governmental ranks and a frontal attack by the Greek armies led by Alexander the Great. In 334 B.C. Alexander entered Asia Minor and defeated Darius III and his armies along the Granicus River. In 333 Alexander broke the back of the remaining Persian armies in eastern Asia Minor at the city of Issus. Alexander then turned southward into Syria and Palestine on his way to conquer Egypt. He entered Egypt without resistance in 332. During this campaign, Judah submitted to the Greek army. The Greeks completed their conquest of the Persian empire in the East beyond the Indus River by 327 B.C.

Historical Geography of Palestine II

In 323 B.C., Alexander died in the city of Babylon. At his death, the major part of the empire he had only just built was divided between two of his generals—Ptolemy, who took Egypt and Palestine, and Seleucus, who took Babylon, Mesopotamia, and Syria. The Ptolemies ruled Palestine from Alexandria, Egypt, for the next one hundred years. In 198 B.C. the Seleucids, under Antiochus III, defeated the Ptolemies and gained control of Palestine.

It was under the brutal reign of the Seleucid king Antiochus IV that civil war broke out among the Jews in Palestine (167 B.C.). That revolt, and its victorious conclusion in 165 B.C., resulted in the establishment of a semi-independent rule of the Hasmonean family, who led the revolt. The chief aim of the Hasmonean rulers was to regain the territory of the ancient kingdom of David. In this, they enjoyed much success.

Internal civil war and the eventual defeat by the Romans in 63 B.C., however, marked the end of the Hasmonean rule. In 40 B.C., the Romans, fearing the Parthians might gain control of Palestine, appointed a local military leader, Herod, son of Herod Antipater, as "king of the Jews." His task was to secure and rule the Roman province of Judea.

Herod, known as Herod the Great, successfully ruled Judea until his death in 4 B.C. His kingdom had two administrative sections: Greek cities, which received considerable autonomy, and Jewish provinces, ruled directly through a network of appointed officials (see next section).

In the latter part of his reign, Herod divided his kingdom into three sections, each ruled by one of his sons: Archelaus ruled Judea and Idumea; Herod Antipas ruled Galilee and Perea; Philip ruled the region northeast of the Jordan River. Archelaus's rule proved too severe by even Roman standards, so that he was deposed by the Roman government in A.D. 6 and replaced by Roman officials. During the ministry of Jesus in Palestine, Judea was governed by a Roman official named Pontius Pilate.

Political World of Palestine in the Time of Jesus

Regarding the two political groups in Palestine, the Greek cities were primarily colonies of soldiers who settled in this region after their term of service was over. These areas were under the direct supervision of the governor of Syria.

The Jewish provinces consisted of various political and geographical regions that had been carved out over the centuries. Herod accepted the ancient division of the region into various provinces and assigned them to his three sons. Archelaus was given the rank of ethnarch, "ruler of a people," while Herod Antipas and Philip received the slightly lesser rank of tetrarch, "ruler of a fourth of a region." Each region was, in turn, divided into "toparchies," or local territories, and each of these was divided into towns and villages.

The province of *Galilee* consisted of four toparchies in Lower Galilee and one in Upper Galilee. Here Jesus spent most of his earthy life. Geographically it consisted of the lands bordering the Sea of Galilee and lying north of the great Valley of Jezreel. Nazareth, the hometown of Jesus, was in Galilee, as was Capernaum, the city where Jesus centered most of his early ministry.

The province of *Perea* was a narrow strip of land east of the Jordan River, stretching from the Dead Sea north to the opening of the Valley of Jezreel. It linked the Jewish province of Judea in the south with the Jewish Galilee in the north. One could travel from Judea to Galilee without passing through Samaria by crossing the Jordan River and taking the route through Perea.

Judea, the central hill country around Jerusalem, was ruled by a Roman official during most of Jesus' time. It was divided into eleven toparchies. Jerusalem itself was administered by a Roman commissioner. In religious and legal questions, decisions in Jerusalem were made by the Jewish Sanhedrin (council of elders).

Idumea was the region south of Judea. Some early historians considered it part of Judea.

Samaria was west of the Jordan River, between Judea and Galilee. It was populated from early times by Samaritans. Much animosity existed between Jews and Samaritans in Jesus' day.

The *northeast region of Palestine* was governed by Philip. It consisted of a loosely defined group of villages and towns inhabited by Jews. In the same region were many independent Greek cities.

The area known as the *Decapolis* (meaning "ten-part city") lay primarily along the eastern plateau of the Transjordan. It also included a small amount of territory west of the Jordan. It consisted of a league of ten Greek cities formed in the early days of Roman occupation of Palestine. These cities were united with common economic, commercial, and military interests.

The total Jewish population of Palestine at the time of Jesus was just under three million.

The Social World of Palestine

With the establishment of the empire of Alexander the Great came a systematic effort to unite all the known world, east and west, into a single Greek-speaking culture. Greek replaced Aramaic as the language of international trade and commerce. Alexander arranged mass marriages between his own troops and the native populations he conquered. He encouraged his soldiers to settle in Greek colonies established throughout his conquered territories, each of which became an active center from which to spread Greek culture.

As the tide of Greek influence began to sweep over the isolated Jewish settlements in Palestine, Jews increasingly faced the challenge of rethinking their traditional values and ideas. What might be the meaning of these ancient traditions when cast into Greek ways of thinking? The answer to this question gave rise to a process within Judaism called Hellenization.

One of the most important steps of Hellenization came during the early reign of Ptolemy (ca. 300 B.C.), when many thousands of Jews were led captive to Egypt and resettled in the Hellenistic city of Alexandria. Those Jews felt great pressure to conform to the Greek culture of that city. These Jews later translated the Hebrew Scriptures into Greek (a translation called the Septuagint), which not only provided a major step in the Hellenization of Judaism, but also opened up the books of the Old Testament to non-Hebrew-speaking people.

A further consequence of the advance of Hellenism among the Jews was the mounting opposition it faced within the ranks of Judaism. Not all Jews viewed the process of Hellenization in a positive light. Some felt it was essential to remain faithful to the ancient traditions. The first stages of this conflict surfaced in the division between the Pharisees and the Sadducees, which forms such an important part of the social structure of the world of the Gospels.

A much more serious confrontation developed with a movement to worship the Greek gods, which formed the basis of the most devastating upheaval during this time, the Maccabean revolt. Jews were literally being asked to give up their most fundamental tenet, the prohibition of idolatry. Some Jews had, in fact, reached the point where they were willing to offer sacrifices to Greek gods at the temple in Jerusalem. Others, such as the elderly priest Mattathias and his sons Judas, Jonathan, and Simon, saw that the time had come to resist such crass syncretism militarily. Though the rebellion ended in political independence for the Jews (165 B.C.), the conflict with Hellenism continued into the early decades of the first century A.D.

A New (Christian) Calendar

The present system of dividing time before and after the birth of Jesus, B.C. and A.D., originated in A.D. 525, when Pope John I commissioned a standard calendar for the Western Church. Prior to this, the calendar had been based on the reign of the Roman emperors, beginning with the founding of the city of Rome. On this new system, Jesus was born Dec. 25, A.D. 1, 754 years from the foundation of the city of Rome. The years before this date were denoted B.C. (Before Christ) and after A.D. (*anno Domini*, "in the year of the Lord").

Since these early dates were set, some adjustments were found necessary. We now know, for example, that Herod the Great died, at the latest, in the year 750 rather than 754 after the founding of Rome. Since Matthew clearly reports that Jesus was born before Herod died, his birth must have been before 750; that is, he was not born in A.D. 1, but in 4 B.C. By the time Herod's dates came to be more accurately understood, it was too late to change the established chronology.

According to Luke 2:1–5, a Roman census was taken sometime immediately before Jesus' birth. That census was most likely taken between 6 and 4 B.C., shortly before Herod's death and sometime before Quirinius became the Roman governor of the whole region of Syria in A.D. 6.

A Chronology of the Time of Jesus*

    Jesus began his ministry about the same time as John the Baptist, that is, in the fifteenth year of the reign of the Roman emperor Tiberius, A.D. 29 (Luke 3:1). He was "about thirty years old" (3:23). He called his first disciples, turned water into wine at the marriage feast in Cana, and traveled to Capernaum.

    In the month of April (Nisan), A.D. 30, Jesus traveled to Jerusalem to celebrate the Passover (John 2:13, 23). He spent the remainder of that year preaching in Jerusalem and throughout Judah. Early in A.D. 31, when John the Baptist was imprisoned, Jesus left Judea and, traveling through Samaria, made his way to Galilee to begin an extensive ministry there.

    There is no record in the Gospels of Jesus' traveling to Jerusalem to celebrate the Passover in A.D. 31, but he did travel to Jerusalem to attend the Feast of Tabernacles in October of that year. He returned to Galilee after the feast and continued his ministry there throughout the remainder of the year and into the next.

    Jesus again traveled to Jerusalem in April 32, to celebrate the Passover (John 6:4). He returned to Galilee and then back to Jerusalem in the fall for the celebration of the Feast of Tabernacles (John 7:2, 10). Returning to Galilee for a short stay, Jesus was again in Jerusalem in December 32 for the Feast of Dedication (John 10:22).

    After that feast, Jesus traveled to Perea (John 10:40–42), where he remained until he returned to Judea to raise Lazarus (11:1–54). He then returned to Ephraim (11:54), Samaria, and Galilee (Luke 17:11), before returning for the last time to Jerusalem (17:11–19:28). Jesus arrived in Jerusalem at the time of the Passover in A.D. 33.

    The day and time of Christ's crucifixion was Passover Friday, A.D. 33, at 9:00 A.M. He died at 3:00 P.M. on that day. On the third day, Sunday, Christ arose from the dead; forty days later he ascended to heaven. The duration of his public ministry was about three and a half years.

    *For this section see Harold W. Hoehner, *Chronological Aspects of the Life of Christ* (Grand Rapids: Zondervan, 1977).

From the Birth of Christ to the Beginning of the First Passover

The Birth of John the Baptist
(Luke 1:5-25, 57-80)

Luke begins his account of the life of Christ with the birth of John the Baptist. Like Jesus, John's birth was announced to his parents by an angel. As with the great prophets and patriarchs of the past (e.g., Abraham and Sarah, Gen. 11:30; Isaac and Rebekah, 25:21; Elkanah and Hannah, 1 Sam. 1:5-20), before his conception, John's mother, Elizabeth, was barren (Luke 1:7). His birth is thus a miraculous sign that God was beginning to work with his people.

John's father, Zechariah, was a priest at the temple in Jerusalem. Luke is aware of his priestly lineage and duly records it to assure the credibility of his office. Both John's mother and his father could trace their lineage back to the first priest, Aaron. Elizabeth was even named after the wife of Aaron (cf. Ex. 6:23; Elisheba in Hebrew is Elizabeth in Greek). Luke further assures us that John's parents were "orthodox" in their keeping of the Lord's commandments. This included Zechariah's participation in the responsibilities of the "priestly division of Abijah."

The angel who appeared to Zechariah was Gabriel, the same one who appeared to Daniel to announce the coming of the Messiah (Dan. 9:21). Gabriel told Zechariah that his wife would bear him a son and that his name would fulfill Old Testament prophecy: He would "go on before the Lord, in the spirit and power of Elijah ... to make ready a people prepared for the Lord" (Luke 1:17; see Mal. 4:5-6). When he asked for a sign of assurance that the angel's words were true, Zechariah was stricken with dumbness. After returning home to his wife at the end of his week of temple service, she indeed did conceive, but, apparently because of her old age, did not announce her pregnancy publicly.

Zechariah and Elizabeth lived in "the hill country of Judea" (Luke 1:39), walking the same roads and scanning the same horizons as the ancient patriarch Abraham and the great king David. Though relatives tried in vain to persuade them to follow the ancient customs and name their child Zechariah, John's parents followed the word of the angel, giving him the name John. It was only after confirming his wife's decision by writing out the words "His name is John," that Zechariah was again able to speak.

The Birth of Jesus
(Matt. 1:1–25; Luke 1:26–56; 2:1–20)

At the time the angel Gabriel visited her to announce the birth of Jesus, Mary, his mother, lived in the small Galilean town of Nazareth. She was pledged to be married to Joseph, a descendant of King David and thus of royal descent. Legally, Joseph and Mary were not yet married, but being "pledged" to each other, they were already considered husband and wife (Luke 1:27). The fact that after her visit with Elizabeth Mary returned "home," suggests she lived with her parents during this betrothal period. Until they were legally and publicly married, Mary remained a virgin (Matt. 1:25; Luke 1:34).

When Joseph learned that Mary was pregnant, he suspected the worst of her and was prepared to divorce her. An angel, however, appeared to him in a dream and revealed to him the nature of Mary's pregnancy and of the child that was to be born to them (Matt. 1:18–25). Joseph thus took Mary as his wife.

The royal lineage of Joseph is fully documented in Matthew 1:1–17. Though heir to the throne of David, Joseph was by trade a humble wood-worker, a carpenter. To be a member of the ancient royal family of David in Palestine at this time had little social or political value, for the Davidic throne had been abolished by the Babylonians nearly six centuries earlier. Theologically, however, being of the house of David was of central importance, for it meant that the promised Messiah might one day be born into his household. In the first century, Jews in Palestine still preserved the ancient records of their family lineage.

The Gospel of Luke records the genealogy of Mary, also tracing her lineage back to David, Abraham, and, ultimately, Adam (Luke 3:23–38). Luke writes that Jesus was, "so it was thought," the son of Joseph (3:23a), meaning that Jesus was, in fact, the son of Mary, not of Joseph, and was thus the grandson of Heli, Mary's father.

As soon as the angel had announced to Mary the expected birth of Jesus, she set out to visit her cousin Elizabeth, now six months pregnant with her son John. Mary appears to have stayed with Elizabeth until the birth of John; she then returned home.

At this time the Roman emperor, Caesar Augustus, began a census throughout his kingdom in preparation for a universal tax he would later impose on his realm. According to the Jewish historian Josephus, such a tax was levied in A.D. 6, when Quirinius was governor of Syria (cf. Luke 2:2). In accordance with this census, Joseph and Mary, being of the lineage of David, were required to register in their hometown, Bethlehem, the birthplace of King David (1 Sam. 16:1). Upon their arrival, the places of lodging and guest rooms were filled, so Mary and Joseph were forced to sleep without proper shelter, under the stars. In such conditions, Mary delivered her son, Jesus, and bedded him in a feedbox adjacent to a nearby pasture.

In the evening of the birth of Jesus, angels appeared to shepherds tending sheep nearby Bethlehem and announced his birth. Leaving their flocks behind, they went to find the child. Nearly a thousand years earlier in the same city, the prophet Samuel was sent to anoint a shepherd in Bethlehem as king over God's people Israel (1 Sam. 16:1–13).

The Infancy of Jesus
(Matt. 2:1–12; Luke 2:21–40)

As good parents wishing to obey the Jewish law, Joseph and Mary circumcised Jesus on the eighth day following his birth (Gen. 17:12). Circumcism was a sign that one was a member of the Abrahamic covenant (17:10). On this occasion, his parents named the child "Jesus," the name given by the angel who announced his birth (Luke 1:31). The name means "Savior."

Thirty-two days later, in accordance with the law, Mary presented herself and her child before the priest at the temple in Jerusalem. According to the Mosaic law (Lev. 12:1–4), a woman who gives birth to a son is considered ceremonially unclean for a period of forty days. She must not touch anything sacred or go to the temple until the time of purification was ended. At the completion of that period, she is to present a year-old lamb for a burnt offering and a young pigeon or dove for a sin offering (12:6).

The law also required that "every firstborn male" be consecrated to the Lord (Ex. 13:2, 12) and redeemed at the price of five shekels of silver (Num. 18:16). With the rise of the priesthood in Israel, the religious duties of the firstborn son were taken over by the priests. A price was therefore to be paid to the priests for their service. According to Jewish law, the firstborn child is presented to the priest by his father as he repeats the brief doxology: "He who has sanctified us with his commandments and has commanded us to redeem the (firstborn) son." The father then turns and says again: "He who has given us life." After that the father pays the five silver shekels to the priest and the ceremony is over.

After Jesus' presentation to the priests at the temple, he was taken into the arms of a devout Jew named Simeon. It was customary in Jerusalem to carry small children during times of worship so that godly men might take them in their arms and bless them. Mary and Joseph were perplexed at the meaning of Simeon's blessing, but he also turned and blessed them, assuring them that this child was destined by God to play a crucial role in the future of God's people Israel (Luke 2:25–35). An old prophetess named Anna also recognized Jesus as the one who would bring redemption to Israel (2:36–38).

After Mary and Joseph returned with Jesus to Bethlehem, certain Magi, or wisemen, from the East came to Jerusalem, seeking "the one who has been born king of the Jews" (Matt. 2:2). In all probability, these Magi were Gentile religious leaders to whom, like Balaam in the Old Testament (Num. 22–24), God had somehow announced the coming of the Messiah.

Being specialists in seeing "signs" in the heavens, presumably they saw a particular and unusual star in their sky (perhaps a comet) and followed where the star seemed to be leading them (Jerusalem). This same "star" also led the Magi to the very house where Jesus was staying.

The Magi learned from the Jerusalem scribes that, according to ancient prophecy, the Messiah was to be born in Bethlehem. They set out to search for him with what they took to be Herod's blessing. Secretly, however, Herod intended to harm the child and sought to find him through the Magi.

Jesus in Egypt (Matt. 2:13–23)

The Magi had paid homage and presented their gifts to Jesus, but they returned to their own country in the East through a route that did not take them back to Jerusalem and Herod. They had been warned in a dream that Herod sought to kill the child. When Herod realized that the Magi had outwitted him and that he could not find the child through them, he issued a cruel and desperate decree to "kill all the boys in Bethlehem and its vicinity who were two years old and under" (Matt. 2:16). Though a heinous atrocity, historians tell us that Herod's decree was by no means the worst of his crimes. On one occasion he even had his own wife and children killed. The fact that he set the age of the boys at "two years old and under" may suggest that considerable time had passed since he first heard of Jesus' birth from the Magi. In any event, Joseph and Mary had already been warned of Herod's plan and escaped to Egypt.

Egypt at this time was home to a large population of Jews. Joseph and Mary perhaps had acquaintances or relatives there. Jews, like most others in the large population centers, spoke Greek in Egypt, and their copies of the Bible were also in Greek. Part of Jesus' early education may have included lessons from the Greek Old Testament. The family of Jesus remained in Egypt at least until Herod died, which may have been only a few months or several years.

Having been told by an angel that Herod had died, Joseph and Mary returned to Palestine. They apparently intended to settle in Judea, near Bethlehem, but hearing that Herod's son still reigned in Judea, they traveled further north to Galilee. There they settled in Nazareth. Though small and provincial, this town was also a gathering point for priests on their way to Jerusalem. There would have been ample opportunity for a young boy like Jesus to hear the great themes of Scripture discussed and debated by the leading scribes of the day. It is therefore of no surprise to hear that when Jesus was taken to the Jerusalem temple at twelve years of age, he was already well-versed in the Scriptures (see next section).

Jesus as a Child in the Temple (Luke 2:41–52)

According to Jewish law, Jesus was not obligated to attend the Passover with his parents until he was thirteen years old. It was customary, however, for younger children to accompany their parents to the temple on holy days to familiarize them with the celebrations that would one day be obligatory. The Gospel of Luke records what was apparently his first visit to Jerusalem.

Luke passes over the events of the Feast of Passover, focusing our attention only on what happened afterwards. Jesus stayed behind when his parents set out for home. When they discovered it, Joseph and Mary immediately returned to Jerusalem and frantically searched for the young boy. When they found him after some time, he was still in the temple courtyard, "sitting among the teachers, listening to them and asking them questions" (Luke 2:46). Luke adds the comment, "Everyone who heard him was amazed at his understanding and his answers."

The thorough knowledge of the Scriptures that the young Jesus exhibited in the temple courtyard suggests that his parents owned their own copy of the Scriptures. It was not uncommon for a family to have their own copy of what we now call the Old Testament in Jesus' day, but it would have been a great expense; thus, possession of such a book indicated a family's great love and value for the Scriptures.

Luke summarizes Jesus' childhood with the comment: "And Jesus grew in wisdom and stature, and in favor with God and men" (Luke 2:52).

The Early Home Life Of Jesus

It is clear from later accounts of Jesus' ministry in the synagogues that he had been taught to read and understand the Hebrew Bible (cf. Luke 4:16–17). It is also clear that Nazareth had a synagogue. It is likely, then, that Jesus received a typical Jewish education as part of his upbringing in Galilee.

Such an education would have included both Bible lessons from his parents and grandparents at home and more formal instruction in Scripture in conjunction with the synagogue in Nazareth (see next section). The responsibility of teaching the Scriptures to young children rested heavily on both parents and grandparents—in Jesus' case, Joseph and his father, Jacob (Matt. 1:16), and Mary's father, Heli (Luke 3:23). It was their task not only to teach children the Scriptures, but to take them to school.

As a young child in first-century Palestine, Jesus would have continued to grow up under the teaching and authority of his parents long after his adolescent years. The modern Jewish practice of marking full adult status by celebrating a bar mitzvah at the age of thirteen was not yet established. But age thirteen for boys and twelve for girls did mark the transition from childhood to adolescence.

Since Jesus' father, Joseph, was a carpenter (Matt. 13:55), it is likely, though not necessary, that Jesus also was trained in that profession. When he was older, Jesus was known to his fellow villagers as a carpenter (Mark 6:3). The occupation of a carpenter in that day consisted primarily of working with wood for all sorts of building projects. Jesus would have been skilled in everything from constructing roofing for private houses to making internal furnishings, such as chairs and tables. The carpenter's trade had special tools: the hammer, chisel, saw, and drill. This trade was part of a large economic network of goods and services in first-century Palestine.

Jewish Education in the Synagogue

The study of the Hebrew Scriptures stood at the center of early Jewish education. All of life—social, religious, legal—centered on the teaching of the Torah. The Scriptures were taught in public worship, at special holidays, and in private and group study. It was not the concern of only an educated elite but of everyone.

Most children in Jesus' day received a formal education at school. Every town and many villages established and maintained a school for its children. Jerusalem alone had several hundred synagogues, each of which had a school for reading Scripture and for studying scriptural tradition. The children entered school when they turned six or seven. But education was not available to everyone. The children of the poor were sometimes not formally educated, though as adults they could avail themselves of the opportunity to learn Scripture in the local synagogue. Such cases were, however, the exception.

Learning elementary Hebrew began with practicing the alphabet on wax tablets. The students were taught to read from small scrolls containing selected verses of the Bible—usually taken from the first chapters of Genesis (creation) and Leviticus (sacrifice). Students went on to practice reading from complete Torah scrolls. The order of study was the order of the books in the Hebrew canon.

Sections of Scriptures that were read from Torah scrolls did not contain vowels. The passages had thus to be memorized. This was often accomplished by singing and chanting. In the regular synagogue service, most passages of the Hebrew Bible were also translated into Aramaic.

A typical student was obliged to complete five years of reading the Hebrew Scriptures. After that, he was instructed in the traditional interpretation of Scripture. During this latter period, he also became skilled at a trade, either at home or with a craftsman. At age twelve or thirteen, gifted boys were sent on to the next level of study under the tutelage of a noted master teacher. One might still advance from there to study with renown biblical scholars and wise men.

John the Baptist, the Messenger
(Matt. 3:3-4; Mark 1:1-6; Luke 3:4-6)

The ministry of Jesus was announced by the sudden arrival of a prophetic voice out of the past, the preaching of John the Baptist. John confronted the people in his day with a call to repentance and preparation for the coming of the Messiah. Like the Messiah who was to follow, John's ministry was short-lived and ended in his tragic death (Mark 6:14–29).

John's ministry began in the "fifteenth year of the reign of Tiberius Caesar " (Luke 3:1; i.e., A.D. 29). While in the desert, John was called by God. His calling appears to have been similar to that of a prophet of God during Old Testament times. Like Elijah, the word of the Lord came to him (Luke 3:2); also like Elijah, his prophetic office was marked by his unusual appearance. He wore hair clothing and a leather belt (Mark 1:6; cf. 2 Kings 1:8). From the moment he was called by God, John began to preach throughout the southern regions of Palestine. He called upon his hearers to receive his baptism in the River Jordan.

The Gospels portray John's ministry against the background of several Old Testament quotations (Ex. 23:20; Mal. 3:1; 4:5; Isa. 40:3). These passages identify him as the fulfillment of the Old Testament promise of a "messenger," who was to come in the days before the Messiah. According to Malachi 4:5, the messenger was to be the prophet Elijah. The Gospel writers understand that to mean that the messenger would be a prophet "like Elijah," in the same way as the Messiah was to be a prophet "like Moses" (cf. Deut. 18:15; 34:10).

The Message of John the Baptist
(Matt. 3:1-2, 5-12; Mark 1:4-8; Luke 3:1-3, 7-18)

Central to John's message was his offer of the forgiveness of sins. John's baptism was "a baptism of repentance for the forgiveness of sins" (Mark 1:4). His words, "I baptize you with water, but he will baptize you with the Holy Spirit" (1:8), should be understood in light of the Old Testament teaching about the messianic kingdom. When God sent the Messiah, he promised to gather the people of Israel, sprinkle them clean with water, and put his Spirit within them (Ezek. 36:24–28). John's task was to prepare the people for the coming of the Messiah.

In carrying out that task, John taught that the kingdom of heaven was near and that Israel should repent and live righteous lives in preparation for it. His message included simple ethical teachings, such as, "The man with two tunics should share with him who has none, and the one who has food should do the same" (Luke 3:11). Tax collectors were admonished to collect no more than what was owed, and soldiers were warned against extortion (3:12–14).

John had a considerably large response to his preaching, at least among the common people. The religious leaders, however, wanted no part in his call for repentance. When some did come out to hear his message, John rebuked them: "Who warned you to flee from the coming wrath?" (Matt. 3:7). He then added, "Produce fruit in keeping with repentance" (3:8), and finally, "The ax is already at the root of the trees" (3:10). They fell back on Israel's claim to be the privileged people of God. But John warned them that no one could claim a right to the Abrahamic promises by mere natural lineage. If God chose to do so, he could raise up children for Abraham from dead stones. The true seed of Abraham would be known by its fruit; they were those who did the same righteous deeds reflected in the life of Abraham.

Many saw in John's ministry the possibility that he might be the Messiah (Luke 3:15). But John moved quickly to dispel such ideas. He knew himself to be the *forerunner* of the Messiah, not the Messiah himself. He was an old covenant prophet sent from God to announce the coming of the new covenant Messiah, thus linking the old and the new.

The Baptism of Jesus
(Matt. 3:13-17; Mark 1:9-11; Luke 3:21-23)

Jesus, apparently identifying with the sinful nation that John was calling to repentance, came to John to be baptized in the Jordan River. The location, a place called Bethany, was probably situated along the Jordan River near the city of Jericho. John and Jesus were cousins and their mothers were close friends. In all probability the two of them not only knew each other, but also knew a good deal about each other. News about John was, of course, widely known. But Jesus' mother was careful to keep what she knew about Jesus to herself (Luke 2:51).

John, however, from afar off recognized Jesus as the "Lamb of God, who takes away the sin of the world" (John 1:29), as he was approaching the Jordan to be baptized. John, in fact, hesitated to baptize Jesus, knowing that his was a baptism of repentance. "I need to be baptized by you," he said. But Jesus insisted, saying to John, "It is proper for us to do this to fulfill all righteousness" (Matt. 3:14-15).

The prior and intimate knowledge that John had of Jesus was not, however, the likely basis of his identification of Jesus as the Lamb of God. God had given him a sign by which he was to recognize the messianic King he had been sent to announce—the anointing of the Holy Spirit. God had told John that the Messiah would be that one on whom the Spirit descended and remained.

John saw the Spirit of God descend on Jesus (Matt. 3:16). As he came up out of the water, the heavens were "torn open," the Spirit descended on him as a dove, and a voice said, "You are my Son, whom I love; with you I am well pleased" (Mark 1:11). With these events and words, Jesus was publicly declared as the Spirit-filled messianic prophet in Isaiah 61:1, the messianic Davidic King in Psalm 2:7, and the servant of the Lord in Isaiah 42:1. This occasion also became the means of introducing Jesus as the Old Testament Passover Lamb, seen as a sacrifice to "take away the sin of the world" (John 1:29).

The Testimony of John (John 1:19-34)

After his baptism, Jesus was led into the desert by the Spirit to be tempted by the devil, while John continued baptizing in the Jordan. During this time a delegation from Jerusalem was sent out to examine him, which consisted chiefly of important religious figures, the priests and Levites. Their main concern was to know if John claimed to be the Messiah. To that question, John gave a resolute reply: "I am not the Christ" (John 1:20).

They then asked, "Are you Elijah?" and John again replied: "I am not." Finally, they asked "Are you the Prophet?" meaning the One promised by Moses in Deuteronomy 18 and 34, that is, the messianic prophet. John again replied, "No."

Having satisfied themselves that John was not making any messianic claims about himself, the delegates continued their questions, still seeking to discover who he claimed to be. John answered to their further questions by identifying himself and his mission with a reference to the Old Testament prophets. He was the "voice in the desert," preparing the way of the Messiah. His water baptism was one of preparation for the Spirit-baptism of the coming Messiah.

The next day John saw Jesus again (John 1:29) and identified him as the one on whom the Spirit had descended at his baptism and as the one whose way he was preparing. The following day (1:35) John pointed Jesus out to two of his own disciples. One of these two disciples was Andrew, Simon Peter's brother (John 1:35-51). The other, though not identified, is usually thought to be John, the presumed author of the Gospel of John.

The Beginning of Jesus' Public Ministry
(John 1:35–51)

The first year of Jesus' ministry was in Judea. For these events we must go to John's Gospel. Jesus' first two disciples were Andrew and, in all likelihood, John, who had been disciples of John the Baptist when they met Jesus. Immediately after that, Andrew sent for his brother Peter and brought him to Jesus, announcing him as the long-expected "Messiah."

Seeing Peter, whose name was Simon, Jesus said to him "You will be called Cephas" (John 1:42). There was no doubt a wordplay in Jesus' original words. "Cephas," in Jesus' native tongue, Aramaic, means "Rock," just as "Peter," in Greek, means "Rock."

The next day, Jesus left the region of the Jordan and traveled to Galilee, accompanied by his three disciples Andrew, John, and Peter. En route to Galilee, Jesus also met and called another disciple, Philip, who was from Bethsaida, the same town as Andrew and Peter were from. Philip in turn found Nathanael and brought him to Jesus. Like Andrew, Philip understood that Jesus was the One about whom the Old Testament Scriptures had prophesied.

The clearest recognition and identification of Jesus among these earlier disciples was that of Nathanael. Even at a distance Jesus recognized Nathanael as "a true Israelite" (John 1:47). When he drew near to Jesus and looked on him, Nathaniel declared, "Rabbi, you are the Son of God; you are the King of Israel" (John 1:49). He recognized that Jesus was a prophet sent by God. Jesus promised him that he would see many more miraculous signs to confirm his calling.

Jesus' First Miracle (John 2:1-13)

Not long after this Jesus performed his first miracle—turning water into wine at a marriage feast in the Galilean city of Cana. Three days after arriving in Galilee, Jesus received word of the marriage of a friend of his family. The wedding was to be held in Cana, a city in central Galilee, just north of Nazareth. Since his mother was already at the wedding, Jesus accepted an invitation to attend.

In the course of the wedding celebration, the host ran out of wine. Having some idea that Jesus may work a miracle, his mother came to him for help. Jesus at first appeared hesitant to reveal his identity by performing a miracle. The time to reveal himself publicly had not yet come, he said. His mother, however, ignoring his refusal, ordered the servants of the marriage host to follow Jesus' every instruction.

Jesus then ordered the servants to fill six stone jars with water. When they had done that, he ordered them to serve the master of the banquet from these same jars. As they carried out his orders and poured from the jars, it was discovered that the water had turned to wine (John 2:1-11). The result of the miracle was to demonstrate his glory as Lord of creation and to strengthened the faith of his disciples with him at the wedding.

Following this marriage celebration, Jesus traveled to Capernaum with his mother and family and his disciples. He remained for several days in Capernaum, which was situated along the western shoreline of the Sea of Galilee (John 2:12). It is not certain what he did during that time. He remained there only a short time, however, because the Passover was nearing and he was soon to set out for Jerusalem to celebrate it there (2:13).

Jesus' Messianic Zeal (John 2:14–25)

Having begun his ministry in the somewhat remote regions of Galilee and primarily in the presence of friends and family, Jesus now turned to Jerusalem, the center of Jewish religious life for over one thousand years. There, in the city of David, he officially announced his coming as the messianic King of Israel. He did this, however, in a subtle and preliminary way—by demonstrating his zeal for the purity of the temple, the house of God. Such a zeal was to be a trademark of the Messiah promised in the Old Testament (cf. 1 Chron. 17:14).

Upon arriving in Jerusalem, Jesus went immediately to the temple, which he found filled with people concerned only about the everyday affairs of business and commerce. Livestock was being sold, and money was being exchanged. Seeing this, Jesus fashioned a cord of rope into a makeshift whip and physically drove the merchants with their wares out of the temple area. "How dare you turn my Father's house into a market!" he taunted the merchants. By this saying, Jesus was claiming to speak and act on behalf of his heavenly Father.

Those present, alarmed and dismayed by Jesus' actions, demanded him to perform a miraculous sign to validate his bold actions. But Jesus replied only with a cryptic reference to his future resurrection: "Destroy this temple, and I will raise it again in three days." Those who heard him thought he was speaking of the Jerusalem temple, but he was, in fact, speaking of his own resurrected body. At the time, the meaning of the remark was lost—even on his disciples. Only after the resurrection did they come to realize that the cleansing of the temple was a picture of a new relationship between God and his people.

The First Passover After Jesus' Baptism (John 3:1–25)

Jesus' cleansing of the temple at the beginning of his ministry was not the only time Jesus did this. Nearly three years later, at the end of his ministry, he again entered Jerusalem, visited the temple, and repeated his actions (Mark 11:15–17). His zeal for the temple had not diminished, nor had the nation's neglect of the temple lessened. The Father's house had been made "a den of robbers" (11:17); Jesus again felt compelled to cleanse it and renew it as a place of worship.

During the celebration of the Passover in Jerusalem, Jesus backed up his messianic claims with numerous "miraculous signs," though the biblical record is not specific about the nature of those signs. Most likely they were similar to the other signs Jesus performed throughout the Gospel accounts. He healed the sick, cast out demons, and demonstrated unequivocal authority over the forces of nature. As a result of these signs, many Jews believed in him as the Messiah.

But Jesus did not attempt to force the issue of his messiahship by appealing to the support of this growing group of believers. He was fully aware that his mission would be accomplished only after Israel's hearts had been cleansed and they had been given new life by the Spirit. The occasion for his own expression of that conviction came when he was secretly visited at night by a high Jewish official, Nicodemus (John 3:1–21). Jesus was surprised that this man, a leader of the Jews, was unaware of the Old Testament teaching of the necessity of a new heart (Ezek. 36:24–26).

As if to heighten Israel's consciousness of the need for a cleansed heart, Jesus left Jerusalem and went into the Judean countryside to begin baptizing with his disciples (John 3:22). John continued to baptize too, witnessing to Jesus as the true One sent from God (3:23–36).

From the First to the Second Passover

Jesus Departs Judea for Galilee

After baptizing for a time in Judea, Jesus left that region to go to Galilee, where the Synoptic Gospels begin their account of Jesus' ministry. Once there, Jesus traveled throughout the region, performing miracles and teaching. The primary focus of the beginning of his Galilean ministry was selecting and building disciples.

The Gospels suggest at least two reasons why Jesus left Judea for Galilee. (1) The Pharisees had heard that Jesus was baptizing more disciples than John the Baptist. Presumably he did not want to give an occasion for them to sow seeds of conflict between his disciples and John's over the issue of who baptized more converts or who was the more successful (cf. John 3:25; 4:1–3). Moreover, by this time the Pharisees were well aware of who Jesus was, and thus they had been given ample opportunity to repent and be baptized.

(2) John the Baptist was at that time thrown into prison (Matt. 4:12; cf. Luke 3:19–20). He had angered the tetrarch of Judea by denouncing publicly Herod's adulterous marriage to his brother's wife. We need not suppose that Jesus was afraid of a similar fate, for there was little chance of him being associated directly as one of John's disciples. But John's arrest may have signaled the fact that conditions in Judea were no longer suitable for the kind of public ministry Jesus intended to carry out (cf. Luke 4:14a).

As Jesus was departing from Judea, he stopped at Jacob's well in Samaria (John 4:4–42). To travel from Jerusalem to Galilee in a direct route, one had to travel through Samaria. In Jesus' day, Jews and Samaritans bore a long-standing animosity toward each other, and it was customary for Jews to avoid traveling through Samaria by going through Perea.

Jesus and his disciples arrived in Sychar, near the ancient city of Shechem (Gen. 33:18–19), at noon. Sending his disciples into the city to purchase food, Jesus remained at the well just outside the city. A Samaritan woman came to draw water, and Jesus spoke to her. Surprised at first that a Jew would speak with her, the conversation quickly turned to the identity of Jesus as the Messiah and to her own personal life. Jesus seemed to know everything about her, including her basic human need for eternal life. When the woman realized that Jesus was the very Messiah her own people, the Samaritans, were eagerly awaiting, she put her trust in him and left to tell those in her village about Jesus. Jesus then stayed two days in Sychar (John 4:40). Many in that city acknowledged Jesus as their Messiah, "the Savior of the world" (4:42).

Ministry in Galilee
(Matt. 4:13-17; Mark 1:14b-15; Luke 4:14b-31; John 4:43-46a)

Jesus was welcomed by the Galileans because they had seen all he had done in Jerusalem at the Passover (John 4:45). He also revisited Cana, the site of his first sign-miracle. There he was met by "a certain royal official whose son lay sick at Capernaum" (4:46). This man appealed to Jesus to heal his son. When Jesus told him his son would live, the official took him at his word and returned to Capernaum. His son was, in fact, healed at the exact time Jesus had said, "Your son will live" (4:53). As a result, the official and all his household believed in Jesus.

Word about Jesus soon spread throughout Galilee. He traveled throughout the region and spoke in numerous synagogues. The typical reception of Jesus and his teaching was overwhelmingly positive there, but that was about to change. Jesus was beginning to announce both his true identity and the reason for which he had come into the world.

To do so in a public manner, Jesus chose his own hometown, Nazareth, and the synagogue in which he had grown up. It was permissible for any member to rise voluntarily to take part in the service. Jesus thus waited for the public reading of Scripture, and when the time came, he made his way to the front. On this particular Sabbath, the scroll of the book of Isaiah was dutifully handed to him. Jesus unrolled it to chapter 61 and began to read, "The Spirit of the Lord is on me, because he has anointed me to preach good news to the poor." Having read these words he rolled the scroll back up, returned it to the attendant, and took his seat.

Sensing the importance of those words and the nature of Jesus' ministry in their own city, all those present sat quietly as Jesus began to speak. He did not give a long, detailed exposition of the passage. His words were, in fact, surprisingly brief. One of the signs of a great teacher in Judaism was the use of few words. Jesus simply stated that the words of this prophecy in Isaiah was on that very day being fulfilled; he was announcing to his own hometown friends and family that he was the long-awaited Messiah spoken of by Isaiah. Whatever they may have thought of him up to now no longer mattered. They were to know him by a new identity.

Those who listened to Jesus were not prepared for such words. They protested that he was one of the hometown boys and that they all knew his father Joseph. But Jesus compared them with the unfaithful Israelites during the days of the prophet Elijah's ministry. The congregation became furious at this suggestion. They rose up against him and, literally, threw him out of town. They even took him to a steep precipice on the edge of town and were prepared to throw him over the side to his death. At the last moment, however, Jesus turned to face the crowd and walked away unscathed (Luke 4:28–30).

Teaching in Capernaum (Matt. 4:13–17)

Leaving Nazareth, Jesus made his way to the city of Capernaum, located in the ancient territorial boundaries of Zebulun and Naphtali. It was in this region of Galilee that the prophet Isaiah had foretold the Messiah would first bring his message of hope and salvation (Isa. 9:1–2). This was the "land of the shadow of death," upon which "a light has dawned."

The narrow escape at the synagogue in Nazareth seems not to have deterred Jesus from continuing his practice of teaching in synagogues. We are not told, however, whether he continued to announce himself openly as the promised Messiah in Capernaum, as he had in Nazareth. It appears, however, that he did not. On one occasion, in fact, he rebuked an "evil spirit" for identifying him as "the Holy One of God" (Luke 4:34). On another occasion, when the demons he had cast out shouted, "You are the Son of God!" Jesus quieted them "because they knew he was the Christ [i.e., the Messiah]" (4:41).

Only gradually did Jesus allow his identity as the promised Messiah to become manifest. Meanwhile, however, he continued to preach and teach in the synagogues throughout the region of Capernaum, and he healed many of their diseases (Luke 4:42–44).

Call of the Disciples
(Matt. 4:18–22; Mark 1:16–28; Luke 4:31–37; 5:1–11)

On his way to Capernaum from Nazareth, Jesus taught many crowds of people in the cities and hamlets of Galilee. As he did so, he called on the people to "repent, for the kingdom of heaven is near" (Matt. 4:17). Reaching the Sea of Galilee, Jesus began to preach to those who had gathered (Luke 5:1). As the crowd pressed in around him, he saw Peter (Simon), Andrew, James, and John washing their nets by the seaside and their boats tied up at the water's edge. Jesus got into Peter's boat and asked him to shove out a short distance from the shore. From there, Jesus continued teaching and preaching to the ever-increasing crowd (5:2–3).

When he had finished speaking, Jesus asked Peter to set sail for the deep waters and let down his nets. Having not caught a single fish the whole of the previous night, Peter only reluctantly did what Jesus said. When he cast his nets out, however, they immediately filled with fish—so much so that he needed help from his partners, James and John (Luke 5:4–10).

This incident made a lasting impression on the fishermen. Peter fell at Jesus' feet and cried, "Go away from me, Lord; I am a sinful man!" In light of that occasion, Jesus called Peter and his associates to be "fishers of men"; they "left everything and followed him" (Luke 5:11).

On the Sabbath following this event, Jesus went to the synagogue at Capernaum and, as was his usual practice, began to teach. He urged his listeners to repent and prepare for the coming kingdom of God. Jesus also healed a man possessed by a demon (an evil spirit). The demon had cried out to Jesus in recognition of him as "the Holy One of God," but Jesus quieted him; he had no need nor desire to be announced by such heralds. The congregation who had heard him teach and who now had seen this display of divine power, were "amazed" and quickly spread the news about Jesus throughout the region.

Further Miracles
(Mark 1:29–39; Luke 4:38–44)

After the Sabbath service at Capernaum, Jesus went to the home of Peter. Though Peter and Andrew were originally from Bethsaida (John 1:44), they now lived in Capernaum, where they were fishermen. In Peter's house, his mother-in-law lay sick with a high fever. Jesus healed her, and she was able to get up from her bed and serve them the midday meal.

As the day came to a close, many others with serious illnesses were brought to Jesus, and he healed them all.

At daybreak the following morning, Jesus left Peter's house and retreated to a solitary place. His intent was clearly to leave Capernaum unnoticed and continue preaching in the other cities and villages of Palestine. When the crowds caught up with him and pleaded with him to remain in Capernaum, Jesus told them that his task was to continue to "preach the good news of the kingdom of God to the other towns" (Luke 4:43). Jesus thus continued to preach throughout both Galilee (Mark 1:39) and Judea (Luke 4:44).

Cleansing a Leper and Healing a Paralytic (Matt. 8:2-4; 9:1-8; Mark 1:40-45; 2:1-12; Luke 5:12-26)

In the Old Testament, leprosy was frequently used by the prophets as a particularly graphic picture of Israel's sin (cf. Isa. 1:6). In Jesus' day it was considered incurable. The power to cleanse a leper was thus a clear sign of miraculous power. When, during his travels through Galilee, Jesus demonstrated such power, huge crowds of people came out to hear him and to be healed of their diseases.

Such popularity with the people aroused concern among the religious leaders—the Pharisees and teachers of the law. They began to follow Jesus and pay close attention to his teaching (Luke 5:17).

On one occasion these religious leaders and teachers were present when Jesus healed a paralytic. Having returned to Capernaum, Jesus was teaching and healing the sick in one of the houses in the city. Finding no way to bring a paralyzed man to Jesus for healing, his friends took him to the top of the house and lowered him on a mat through the tiled ceiling. Seeing such faith, Jesus immediately forgave the man of his sins. Surprised and perplexed, the Pharisees considered this an act of blasphemy. They knew quite well that only God can forgive sins (Luke 5:21). Knowing their thoughts and wanting to show these religious leaders that he had indeed come from God, Jesus healed the paralytic man right before their eyes.

The response of the entire crowd was amazement and praise. Nothing like this had ever been seen in their day. Even the Pharisees and teachers of the law were amazed at what they saw. Apparently they too were among those who praised God for what they had seen (Mark 2:12).

The Call of Levi (Matthew)
(Matt. 9:9-13; Mark 2:13-17; Luke 5:27-32)

Jesus added to the number of his disciples by calling a Jewish tax collector in Capernaum. Levi (also called Matthew) had set up a collection booth by the shore of the Sea of Galilee. His job was the unpopular one of assigning and collecting taxes for the Roman government. He was working for the enemy! He was a wealthy man with influential friends. All this he left behind when Jesus called him to be a disciple.

Matthew prepared a great feast and invited all his friends and associates to dine with Jesus. The fact that Jesus accepted this invitation led to a serious concern from the Pharisees and the teachers of the law about just who Jesus claimed to be. That concern came in the form of a question about fasting. Fasting (going without food and drink for a designated period of time) was a sign of devotion to God and a striving for purity. It was usually prescribed as a way to prepare for some momentous event, such as a religious festival (e.g., the annual Day of Atonement, Lev. 16:29; see also Ex. 34:28). Both the Pharisees and the disciples of John the Baptist adhered strictly to the rite of fasting.

People such as Levi, however, were known for the "eating and drinking," which was anything but fasting. Jesus explained this apparent anomaly with an analogy from everyday life, a wedding celebration. A wedding is a time of celebration, not a time of fasting. Jesus' presence among his disciples was like that of a bridegroom at a wedding. His friends rejoice with him at the wedding, but later, when he is taken away from them in marriage, they will miss his company and long to see him again. In the same way, Jesus said, his own disciples had no reason to fast while he was with them. But the time would come when they would have to wait in anticipation and preparation for his return. At that time his disciples would also fast. Jesus went on to explain his mission as one that called sinners to repentance.

Plucking Grain on the Sabbath
(Matt. 12:1–8; Mark 2:23–28; Luke 6:1–5)

On a Sabbath day, Jesus was journeying with his disciples through the grain fields, and his disciples began to pick some of the grain and rub it together to eat. Immediately, the Pharisees interpreted it as a breech of the Sabbath laws. It was forbidden to "work" on the Sabbath; the disciples, they insisted, were "working" because they were picking grain and rubbing kernels together to eat. Jesus defended the actions of his disciples by appealing to the Old Testament story of David's fleeing from Saul. At that time David's men ate bread that had been consecrated for the priests. Jesus did not attempt to defend the actions of his disciples as "lawful." He rather defended them for their understanding of the real purpose of the Sabbath and for their awareness that the "Lord . . . of the Sabbath" was with them.

As a further explanation of the difference between the customs of Jesus' disciples and those of the Pharisees and John, Jesus taught the lesson of new garments and new wineskins. One does not patch up an old, worn-out piece of clothing with a new cloth. The new cloth will cause the old to rip and make matters worse. The new does not mix well with the old. The same was true, Jesus taught, with new wine in old wineskins. The new wine will burst if put into old wineskins.

John and the Pharisees represented the old ways. Their disciples had to carry out the customs and practices of the old ways. But Jesus' disciples had to live according to the new ways that God had initiated in sending Jesus. A time for fasting would come when he was taken away, but for the present, a time of celebration, there was no place for the kind of mourning and anticipation that accompanied fasting.

The Second Year
of Jesus' Ministry

Jesus' Second Passover (John 5)

At this time Jesus traveled to Jerusalem "for a feast of the Jews" (John 5:1). Much discussion has centered on whether this feast was, in fact, a Passover. While a conclusive decision cannot be reached, most likely it was. While there, Jesus became involved in yet another incident that raised afresh the question of the meaning and continuing validity of the Sabbath.

In Jerusalem was a pool of water called Bethesda, which means "place of kindness." It was built as a sort of public bath, surrounded by large colonnades. Since it was near the Sheep Gate, it may have been used originally for watering or washing sheep brought to the temple. In Jesus' day it had become a gathering place for those who believed in the special healing powers of its waters. An early and widely circulated story associated with this pool told of an angel who would come and stir up the waters of the pool so that "the first one into the pool after each such disturbance would be cured of whatever disease he had" (John 5:4; see NIV note; cf. the invalid's words to Jesus in 5:7).

Jesus was drawn to an aged invalid, who had waited thirty-eight years to be healed by its waters. By the mere power of his spoken word, Jesus healed the man and said, "Get up! Pick up your mat and walk." By obeying the command, the invalid inadvertently broke one of the Jewish Sabbath laws, which forbade one to carry something on the Sabbath. When confronted by the religious authorities, the man's only explanation was that the person who had healed him also commanded him to take up his mat and walk. Later, after he had learned who had given him this command, the invalid returned to the religious authorities and told them about Jesus.

This was one of many instances of Jesus' doing miraculous works on the Sabbath. Because of such works the religious leaders began to persecute him. To make matters worse, when Jesus tried to explain his actions, he claimed a higher authority than Jewish law—he claimed to be doing the work of God, his Father, which superseded the requirements of the Sabbath law. Some Jews even sought to kill Jesus for such claims. Jesus, however, held his ground. He appealed to his miraculous works as a sure sign that God had indeed sent him. He also appealed to the Old Testament Scriptures. The Jews, he argued, had set their hopes on the laws contained in the writings of Moses. Jesus admonished them to take a closer look at those Scriptures. If they truly understood what Moses had written, they would believe in him.

Return to Galilee
(Matt. 12:9–14; Mark 3:1–6; Luke 6:6–11)

Some time after the Passover feast, Jesus returned to Galilee, where he was about to embark on a major part of his mission. Besides his many miraculous works, he chose his twelve disciples, taught them, and sent them out to carry on his work. The Gospels contain many individual accounts of Jesus' actions during this period. They are not always arranged chronologically in each of the Gospels, but they fall rather neatly into a general historical pattern.

One of Jesus' first actions back in Galilee was to attend a synagogue in Capernaum. There he saw a man with a withered hand. By this time, the issue of whether Jesus should heal someone on the Sabbath had begun to follow him, and it overshadowed his other great acts of divine power. All eyes at the synagogue turned to see whether Jesus would now heal the man. Certainly this illness could wait until the next day; thus, it proved to be an ideal test case of Jesus' authority over the Sabbath.

The Pharisees were, in fact, using the issue of Sabbath observance as an excuse to find some accusation against Jesus (Mark 3:2). When Jesus saw this, he was angered and grieved. But he was determined not to let it hinder his work, and so he commanded the man to stretch out his hand—and he was healed. That was all the Pharisees were looking for. They immediately went out of the synagogue and met with a caucus of powerful political leaders, the Herodians. Their intent was to draw up plans to destroy Jesus.

More Healings and Choosing the Twelve
(Matt. 12:15–21; Mark 3:7–19; Luke 6:12–16)

After the service at the synagogue, Jesus and his disciples went out to the shore of the Sea of Galilee. A great crowd of people followed them. By now the crowd consisted of more than merely curious local onlookers. In it were people from virtually every region of the Near East: Galilee, Judea, Jerusalem, Idumea, the Transjordan, and Tyre and Sidon. News of Jesus had spread far and wide. He had healed many, and many more had come to be healed.

As he taught the burgeoning crowd, "evil spirits" often cried out to him as "the Son of God." Jesus rebuked them, however, and warned them not to reveal his true identity. He was not willing to be announced by such messengers; their testimony was not worthy of his honor. Jesus also was concerned that the crowds see his works and draw their own conclusions as to his identity. He wanted his works to speak for themselves.

The time had now come for Jesus officially to choose twelve representatives and send them out to preach the Gospel. Their task was to proclaim Jesus as the Messiah, who had come to establish the promised eternal kingdom of David (cf. 2 Sam. 7:16). Retreating to the mountainous region of Galilee, Jesus summoned twelve of his followers and commissioned them as his official apostles, or "sent ones." He gave them authority to preach and to cast out demons.

The twelve apostles were: Simon (Peter), James (the son of Zebedee), John (the brother of James), Andrew, Philip, Bartholomew, Matthew (Levi), Thomas, James (the son of Alphaeus), Thaddaeus, Simon (the Zealot), and Judas Iscariot.

The Sermon on the Mount
(Matt. 5–7; Luke 6:17–49)

Jesus taught his disciples extensively. He also taught the huge crowds that gathered around him. They came largely to be healed and to see a miracle, but Jesus always saw to it that they got more than they came for. They received a lesson in how to walk with God and prove faithful to his Word. Both Matthew and Luke record summary accounts of a typical "sermon" preached by Jesus. Matthew's account is situated on a mountainside and is thus traditionally called the Sermon on the Mount. Luke's account is situated on a "level place" and is thus usually taken to be a record of essentially the same sermon preached on a different occasion.

Much debate has centered around the meaning and application of Jesus' sermon today. Some suggest his message as summarized in the Sermon on the Mount expresses the essence of the gospel. Others elevate the sermon in importance over the work of Christ on the cross. Still others suggest that Jesus' sermon is to be understood today as a summation of the way of life of those who have put their faith in Christ's finished work on the cross. That is, the Sermon on the Mount represents how a Christian should live as a Christian, not how a sinner becomes a Christian. The generally optimistic and perfectionist viewpoint of Matthew 5–7 has led still others to suppose that its message is not for Christians today, but for those in the future who will live during the time of Christ's kingdom here on earth. Such a view has the merit of taking seriously the fact that Jesus taught his sermon to those of the household of Israel and that its context was the establishment of the promised Old Testament kingdom. To hold such a view, however, overlooks the important fact that in writing his Gospel, Matthew includes the sermon. That can only mean that he expected it to apply to his readers, those in the New Testament church.

Further Healings
(Matt. 8:1–13; Luke 7:1–10)

Immediately after his sermon on the mountainside, Jesus returned to Capernaum. En route he was met by a leper, who begged to be healed. Jesus had compassion on the man. Before the eyes of the entire crowd, he said, "Be clean!" (Matt. 8:3), and the leper was instantly healed. Jesus warned him not to publicize what had happened to him, but rather to show himself to the priests in Jerusalem, as the biblical law required. It was their responsibility to determine whether his leprosy was truly gone. Only then could he truly be pronounced healed.

As he entered Capernaum, Jesus was met by a group of leaders from the town, asking him to come to the home of a Roman centurion. The centurion's servant was gravely ill, and he wanted Jesus to heal him. The town leaders told Jesus how important the centurion was to them, for he had contributed greatly to the building of their synagogue.

As Jesus drew near to the centurion's home, the man sent word that Jesus should come no further. It was enough that he speak a word and heal his servant. He did not feel worthy for Jesus to come to his house. The centurion recognized that Jesus had authority and power to heal his servant without coming to him in person, and Jesus saw in the centurion's request an expression of genuine faith. That was, in fact, a quality of faith that Jesus had not seen in his own people's response to him. Jesus also saw in the centurion's faith a picture of the many Gentiles who would receive him, in contrast to the many Jews who would reject him.

Jesus and His Family
(Matt. 12:46–50; Mark 3:21, 31–35; Luke 8:19–21)

Reports about Jesus had by now spread throughout the region. The crowds that gathered to see and hear him were becoming large. Jesus was so preoccupied with them that he, literally, had no time to eat and rest. Apparently worried about his well-being, members of his family, and perhaps some of his friends, came to Jesus, wanting to take him away for a rest.

At a later time in Capernaum, Jesus' mother and brothers paid him another visit. When they arrived, the crowd was so large they could not get in. They apparently were not worried about his well-being this time; rather, they wanted to visit with him as a son and as a brother. Jesus used the occasion to distance himself from them. His family apparently represented to him the everyday concerns of life, which can weigh down one who has an important task or calling. Jesus' concern lay in the individuals who stood and sat before him in the crowds. They, not his family and friends, were the ones he had come into the world to seek and to save. They had, in fact, become his "family." Such a family consisted of all those present with him, not merely his earthly mother and brothers.

We must be careful how we interpret Jesus' response to them. The Scriptures do not say he did not happily receive them. Presumably he did. Jesus' main concern, however, was to teach the greater spiritual truth that those who follow him and keep his words are like his own family.

The mention of the brothers of Jesus reminds us that Mary and Joseph had other children besides Jesus. Some of them, in fact, did not believe in him—at least, not at this time (John 7:5). The names of Jesus' brothers were James, Joses (Joseph), Judas, and Simon; Jesus also had sisters (Mark 6:3). The fact that Joseph is not mentioned need not lead us to conclude that he had, by then, died, though there is nothing to suggest he had not.

A Widow and Her Son, and a Question from John (Matt. 11:1–19; Luke 7:11–35)

Jesus continued to travel to towns and villages throughout Galilee. On one occasion, while he was approaching the village of Nain, near Nazareth, he came across a funeral procession for the only son of a widow in that village. This widow was an important person in the city as could be seen by the large crowd accompanying the funeral. When Jesus saw the widow, he first comforted her and then went up to her son's coffin and raised him from the dead. The crowd, filled with awe at what they had just seen, began to spread the word throughout Galilee and Judea that God had done a great deed and had come to help his people.

By now, John the Baptist had been imprisoned. His disciples, however, kept him informed about Jesus and the growing impact of his ministry. Remaining true to his call, John sent two of his disciples to question Jesus and determine from him whether he was truly the expected Messiah. When they put their question to Jesus, he answered with a appeal to Old Testament prophecies (cf. Isa. 35:5–6; 61:1). He told them in no uncertain terms that he was indeed the one of whom Isaiah spoke; he was performing all the "signs" foretold by Isaiah, such as healing the sick, raising the dead, and preaching good news.

Jesus also used the occasion to give the crowd an explanation of the role John had played as the prophet preparing the way for the Messiah. Those who accepted his message and prepared themselves for the Messiah's coming gladly received Jesus' message as well. Those who rejected John and his baptism also opposed Jesus.

Woes Pronounced and the Weary Called
(Matt. 11:20–30; Luke 7:36–50)

Having been identified by John as the one announced by the ancient Hebrew prophets, Jesus proceeded to give a prophetic word of warning of his own to the cities of Galilee. Had the works he was now doing been done in the Gentile cities of Tyre and Sidon, he said, they would have gladly repented. The city of Capernaum had seen great works of God wrought in their midst, but they had not repented and turned to God. A time of great judgment awaited them—one more severe, in fact, than that which overcame the cities of Sodom and Gomorrah.

At this same time Jesus expressed his awareness of the basic character of those who would receive his message. They would not be the wise and intelligent of his generation. Rather, they would be those who, like infants, were willing to put simple faith in their heavenly Father. They would be the weary of this world, who were fully aware of their need of a redeemer. These people would be willing to take Jesus' gentle yoke upon themselves and learn from him.

Another event happened that provided a clear illustration of the kind of followers whom Jesus sought. Jesus was invited to the home of an important, and no doubt wise and intelligent, Pharisee named Simon. While reclining at his table for a meal, a sinful and repentant woman came to the house to see Jesus. (This woman, incidentally, was likely not Mary, the sister of Lazarus and Martha, though a similar thing did happen with her; see John 11:2.) Weeping uncontrollably, the woman washed Jesus' feet with her tears and, with an alabaster jar of perfume, began to anoint his feet.

The Pharisee wondered why Jesus did not recognize her as a sinner. If he were a prophet, would he not know who she is? Jesus, however, knew fully well who the woman was, that she had sinned greatly but now rejoiced over the grace of God that she had found in Jesus. Overcome by her gratitude and humility, he saw her as one who stood in stark contrast to Simon, who had not even offered Jesus the simplest courtesy of supplying him with water to wash his feet when he entered his house.

Further Travels Throughout Galilee
(Luke 8:1-3)

Jesus continued to travel throughout the towns and villages of Galilee, preaching his message about the kingdom of God. The twelve apostles traveled with him, as did several women, such as Mary Magdalene, Joanna, and Susanna. These women provided for Jesus and the disciples out of their own resources. Joanna was considerably wealthy, being the wife of Cuza, a high official in the court of Herod Antipas.

At the conclusion of their travels, Jesus and his followers returned to Capernaum. There they met with considerable opposition from the religious leaders. This was a crucial turning point in Jesus' ministry, marking a decisive break between him and the nation of Israel in his day. Many have suggested that the rejection of Jesus by the religious leaders at this time constituted an official rejection of Jesus as the Messiah. There would be other opportunities offered to the people to accept Jesus as the promised Messiah, but the resistance manifested in the Pharisees' rejection of him on this occasion proved fatal, if not final, for the nation as a whole.

Conflict with the Pharisees
(Matt. 12:22-45; Mark 3:20-30)

The occasion for the Pharisees' infamous rejection of Jesus was his healing a blind mute who was also demon-possessed. When the crowds saw his power, demonstrated by this miracle, they raised the inevitable question, "Could this be the Son of David"? This was the first time that the title "Son of David" was used of Jesus during his ministry. Its use here shows a full awareness of the significance of his ministry: Jesus was the promised Son of David, whose kingdom was to be rebuilt and who would reign in Jerusalem. The people were thus, in fact, asking whether Jesus was the Messiah. In what can only be described as a desperate attempt to stave off such a conclusion, the Pharisees offered an alternative explanation: "It is only by Beelzebub, the prince of demons, that this fellow drives out the demons" (Matt. 12:24).

Jesus responded to their charge with two lines of argument. (1) He exposed the faulty logic of the Pharisees' charge: "If Satan drives out Satan," he said, "he is divided against himself. How then can his kingdom stand?" (Matt. 12:26). Jesus continued, "If I drive out demons by Beelzebub, by whom do your people drive them out?" The point of Jesus' statements was (a) to uncover the important underlying assumption of the Pharisees—Jesus did, in fact, wield supernatural power; and (b) to show their misuse of that assumption—Jesus, like the Pharisees' own exorcists, waged war against the powers of Satan.

(2) Jesus warned the Pharisees against the very conclusion they had drawn: "If I drive out demons by the Spirit of God, then the kingdom of God has come upon you" (Matt. 12:28). The power that the Pharisees acknowledged to be real, was, in fact, a demonstration of the presence of the kingdom of God in their midst. If they rejected that kingdom, Jesus warned, there would be no hope for them. But rejection is precisely what the Pharisees, as a group, persisted in doing. It was becoming clear that the religious leaders of the day, and the nation as a whole, would continue to reject the kingdom Jesus offered. Consequently, Jesus began to teach his disciples, in parables, what would become of the kingdom he had come to establish.

Parables Taught by the Seashore
(Matt. 13; Mark 4; Luke 8:4–18)

On the same day as his family visited him in Capernaum, Jesus went out by the seashore to teach the crowds. Such a large crowd had gathered that he had to sit in a boat just off the shore. Although Jesus often taught his disciples many parables, only seven have been preserved from his teaching on this occasion, each of which makes a particular contribution to the nature of the kingdom of God and its full realization in the future. Each parable centers around the same basic truth: Jesus came to establish the kingdom promised in the Old Testament prophetic literature, and he was, in fact, about to fulfill that mission.

That kingdom, which was to be a visible, universal rule of the Messiah, would begin in a small, almost imperceptible, form, as a mustard seed or a piece of yeast in a lump of dough. Unlike what may have been anticipated from reading the Old Testament Scriptures, there was to be a delay between the coming of the King and the consummation of the kingdom. During that delay, members were to live in expectation of the return of the King and the final establishment of his kingdom at "the end of the age" (Matt. 13:39–40, 49).

That this was a fulfillment of the Old Testament hope in a way that differed from what might have been expected is suggested by Jesus' remarks at the close of his teaching: "Every teacher of the law who has been instructed about the kingdom of heaven is like the owner of a house who brings out of his storeroom new treasures as well as old" (13:52). His view of the kingdom had elements that were a part of the Old Testament's view and some that were new.

From this time on, Jesus taught exclusively in parables, in order to fulfill what the prophets before him had promised. From the time of the ancient prophets, parables were the form in which God had spoken to his people. When the Messiah came, the prophets taught, he too would speak in parables. Through parables the depths of God's truth were communicated to those who believed and concealed from those who did not believe (Matt. 13:11–17).

That parables were often difficult to understand, even by the faithful, is shown by the fact that Jesus was obliged to explain his parables privately to the disciples after he had taught them publicly (Mark 4:33–34).

Crossing the Sea
(Matt. 8:18–27; Mark 4:35–41; Luke 8:22–25)

After a considerable time teaching on the western shores of the Sea of Galilee in and around Capernaum, Jesus made plans to travel with his disciples to the other side of the sea. As they set sail, he found a place in the stern of the boat and fell asleep. While he slept, a great storm arose over the sea, and the disciples feared that the boat would break apart and sink. Water was already filling up the boat.

The disciples abruptly roused Jesus from his sleep and with great alarm pressed him to do something to save them. But they were not expecting what he did next. Speaking directly to the storm, Jesus said simply, "Quiet! Be still!" He treated the wind and the storm as something under his command. Immediately the wind obeyed his voice; the storm died down and the sea grew calm. This is one of the greatest miracles in the Gospels, and the disciples quickly realized that even the wind and seas obeyed Jesus.

The Gadarene Demoniac
(Matt. 8:28–34; Mark 5:1–21; Luke 8:26–39)

After quieting the raging sea, Jesus and his disciples continued until they reached the shoreline of the region of Gerasenes, the region surrounding the ancient city of Geras, east of the Jordan River. As he stepped off the boat, Jesus was immediately confronted by a deranged, demon-possessed man who inhabited the graveyard of a local village. There were, in fact, two such men, but the biblical narratives concentrate on only one of them.

When Jesus commanded the demon to leave the man, he called out to Jesus, begging for mercy. Jesus asked the man his name, but the demons who possessed the man answered that they were not just one, but many in number; hence, the demon called himself "Legion" (a word for a unit of some 12,000 soldiers in the Roman army). They begged Jesus not to cast them "into the Abyss" (Luke 8:31) but to let them go into a large herd of pigs feeding nearby. Jesus granted the demons their request. They entered the herd of pigs and hurled them down a steep embankment and into the sea. The entire herd was drowned.

Having heard of this strange occurrence, the local townspeople came out to investigate. They found Jesus and the notorious, demon-possessed man sitting together peacefully. To their great surprise the man was completely restored, and they became afraid. They saw the power of God demonstrated in Jesus' actions and could not comprehend what it meant for them. They pleaded with Jesus to leave their village, fearing his great power. Jesus offered little resistance to their request. He and his disciples set out in their boat to return to Capernaum. But Jesus would not allow the man who had been healed of demons to follow him back across the sea. Instead, he sent him away, telling him to tell his own countrymen what Jesus had done for him.

Healing of Jairus's Daughter and Woman with the Issue of Blood
(Matt. 9:18–26; Mark 5:22–43; Luke 8:40–56)

Though many religious leaders had by now rejected Jesus and his implicit claims to be the expected Messiah, his authority over sickness and death was widely acknowledged. On his return to Capernaum, Jesus was met by an important synagogue official named Jairus. Falling at his feet, he pleaded with Jesus to come and lay his hands on his dying daughter— believing that she would be well and live if Jesus so willed. Jesus went off with Jairus immediately.

En route to Jairus's home, Jesus was joined by a large crowd. As he worked his way through them, a woman afflicted with a chronic hemorrhaging reached out to touch the edge of his clothing. The exact nature of her illness is purposefully not explained. In ancient medical terms it could have been any of a number of illnesses. That it was a blood disease and likely made her "unclean" in the eyes of the religious leaders seem certain, though it does not appear as if anyone else knew of her affliction. The woman believed she would be healed if she could only touch Jesus' clothing. When she did so, she was immediately healed.

Knowing he had been touched by the woman, Jesus turned to the crowd thronging around him and asked, "Who touched me?" The disciples misunderstood Jesus' question. The woman, however, knew precisely what he meant, and she immediately began to tell her story to Jesus. All this, no doubt, delayed Jesus' primary purpose—to go to Jairus's home to heal his dying daughter.

While Jesus was still talking to the woman, news reached Jairus that his daughter had died. Jesus, calling on Jairus to have faith, went without further delay to his house and into the room where the daughter lay. He attempted to quiet the mourners by telling them that the young girl had not died; she was only sleeping. Those who had gathered to mourn the young girl began to laugh at Jesus. Putting them all out of the house, Jesus turned to the young girl and, taking her hand, said, *"Talitha koum!"* (i.e., "Little girl, I say to you, get up!"). At that, the girl arose and began to walk. When the mourners saw the girl, they were astounded.

Jesus again warned those present not to spread news of this miracle. But it was of no avail. The report of Jesus' miracle quickly spread and became known throughout Galilee.

Capernaum and Nazareth
(Matt. 9:27–34; 13:53–58; Mark 6:1–6a)

When Jesus left the home of Jairus, he was met by two blind men, who cried out loudly, "Have mercy on us, Son of David!" They were acknowledging Jesus as the messianic descendant from the line of David. Jesus asked them whether they had faith in him. When they testified to it, he healed their blindness. This healing exhibits a specific kind of faith. Being blind, these men could not see whom they were to believe in; they could only believe in what they had heard. They thus represented the multitudes throughout Galilee and Judea who never saw Jesus and his works. Having received their sight, these two men went throughout the district spreading the news of what Jesus had done for them.

After a lengthy stay in Capernaum, Jesus departed for more travels and preaching throughout Galilee. His travels led him back to his hometown in Nazareth (Mark 6:1), where he again taught in his own family's synagogue. He found a mixed response there. Many were amazed at his wisdom and miracles, but they could not understand from where he had received such powers. They knew him as a mere carpenter, the son of Mary, who had grown up in their own midst. They thus took offense at what his miraculous works seemed to suggest. They were unprepared to credit him with any authority or importance beyond what they had already come to place in him as a boy growing up in their midst.

This attitude curiously reflected the prophecy in Isaiah about the messianic Servant of the Lord: "He had . . . nothing in his appearance that we should desire him. . . . We esteemed him not" (Isa. 53:2–3). Jesus himself saw Nazareth's response as a result of their lack of faith. A prophet is without honor in his own country. Consequently, he did only a few miracles there. His miracles were intended to strengthen the faith of those who believed in him, not to create faith where there was none. Jesus thus left his hometown disappointed in their response but committed to continue to preach throughout the rest of Galilee.

The Sending of the Twelve
(Matt. 9:37–10:42; Mark 6:8–11, 30–31;
Luke 9:1–6, 10a)

By now Jesus had completed his mission of traveling throughout the villages of Galilee to preach the message of the kingdom of God. His many miraculous works had attracted large crowds, and he was well known throughout the region. Now it was time to commission the twelve apostles to go out also and proclaim the same message.

Jesus sent them out in groups of two. Each group was to take along no provisions for their journey—no walking staff, no food, no money, no knapsack, no extra clothing. They were to depend on the good graces of the people in the towns they visited. If there was no response from a town, they were to leave that town and go on to another. Jesus gave them power over evil spirits and enabled them to heal the sick by anointing them with oil. The message they were to preach was the approaching establishment of the kingdom of God in their midst.

Jesus instructed the apostles to go only to "the lost sheep of Israel"; they were to avoid the Gentiles and the Samaritans (Matt. 10:5). This was because their message dealt with the fulfillment of the Old Testament promises made to the people of Israel. Jesus was here offering the nation the kingdom promised to David. He clearly believed it was fully possible that the nation of Israel would hear the message of these apostles and turn to God. The result would be the establishment of the long-awaited messianic kingdom. But Jesus also believed that the nation might not respond to the message of the apostles and that they would suffer great persecution. The choice lay both in the response of the people of Israel and in the sovereign will of God.

When the apostles returned, they reported all that had happened on their missions (the biblical record is silent about the specifics of their report). That they had good success is evident from the fact that great crowds of people continued to gather around Jesus.

The Murder of John the Baptist
(Matt. 14:3–12; Mark 6:17–29; Luke 9:7–9)

While the apostles were on their mission, preaching the approach of the kingdom, the forerunner of that kingdom, John the Baptist, was put to death. During Jesus' earlier ministry in Judea, John had been imprisoned by Herod Antipas, who had ruled Galilee and Perea after his father appointed him to that position in 4 B.C. According to early historians, John was held at Machaerus, one of Herod's southern fortresses. John had rebuked Herod the tetrarch "because of Herodias, his brother Philip's wife," and all the other evil things he had done (Mark 6:17).

Some time later, Herod held a feast to celebrate his birthday, attended by leading military and political leaders. At the feast, Herodias's daughter danced before the company and pleased Herod so much that he hastily vowed to grant her any wish. Having been advised by her mother, who hated John the Baptist, the daughter requested John's head. Although Herod realized his promise had been foolish, there was no way out. He fulfilled his vow and, in a gruesome scene, had John's head brought on a platter. When John's disciples heard of this atrocity, they claimed his body and buried it.

As the news of Jesus' deeds and miraculous works began to circulate and eventually make their way to Herod's attention, Herod, in his confused state of mind, believed the reports to be about John the Baptist rather than Jesus. Perhaps John had been raised from the dead. Some had, indeed, reported to him that it was John. Herod thus sought Jesus to see if he was, in fact, the John he had murdered. Jesus, however, continued to elude his grasp.

The Third Year
of Jesus' Ministry

Feeding the Five Thousand
(Matt.14:14–21; Mark 6:32–44; Luke 9:10b–17; John 6:1–15)

Great crowds continued to gather around Jesus, so that he had to seek refuge with his disciples in the hill country near Bethsaida, east of the Sea of Galilee. But even that measure gave little relief, for the people continued to follow them, traveling on foot around the sea. Jesus welcomed the people, taught them about the kingdom of God, and healed the sick.

As the day wore on and the people had not brought provisions for food, the disciples came to Jesus with a request that he send the people away to buy food for themselves. Jesus, however, told the disciples to provide food for the crowd themselves. Having gathered only five loaves of bread and two fish from the people, the disciples were perplexed over what Jesus could mean. Did he mean for them to purchase food for the whole crowd?

Taking the five loaves and two fish, however, Jesus blessed it and began distributing portions of food to the crowds through his disciples. In a scene reminiscent of Moses' giving manna to the Israelites in the desert (Ex. 16:4–19) and of the miracles of Elisha (2 Kings 4:1–7, 42–44), the people ate until they were full and even had some left over. The size of the crowd was five thousand men, in addition to the women and children. The crowd concluded that Jesus was indeed the messianic prophet sent from God to establish his kingdom (John 6:14–15).

Jesus' Walking on the Water
(Matt. 14:22–36; Mark 6:45–56; John 6:16–25)

After feeding the five thousand, Jesus put his disciples into their boat at Bethsaida and sent them off to row back to Capernaum, on the other side of the Sea of Galilee. He himself, however, remained behind to dismiss the crowds and to pray in solitude on the mountain.

As evening came, Jesus went down to the shore and saw the disciples' boat battling the heavy winds in the midst of the sea. In the early hours of the morning, Jesus himself set out to return to Capernaum, walking across the storming waters of the sea. When his disciples saw him, they thought it was a ghost. Jesus immediately identified himself.

Peter, still uncertain that it was Jesus, called out to invite him to come to Jesus. Hearing Jesus calling him, Peter climbed out of the boat and onto the raging waters of the sea. At first, with his eyes fixed on Jesus, he walked steadily toward him on the water. When his eyes began to look away from Jesus and toward the threatening waters, Peter's feet began to sink into the waves. In desperation he called out to Jesus, and Jesus took him by the hand and led Peter back safely to the boat.

As Jesus climbed into the boat, the stormy winds that had tossed all night suddenly ceased. His disciples had still not yet fully understood Jesus' true identity. They were astonished, both at his walking on the water and his calming of the sea. Their minds had not grasped the full implications of the miraculous signs he performed. Now, however, safely aboard the boat and seeing the calm sea around them, the disciples began to worship Jesus as the Son of God.

When Jesus arrived at the shore, the villagers at Gennesaret recognized him and spread the word that Jesus was back. Many others had also followed Jesus back across the sea in boats from Bethsaida. When they heard that Jesus was traveling toward this town or that village, they brought their sick to him to be healed. Even those who merely touched his clothing were healed.

Discourse on the Bread of Life (John 6:26–59)

Arriving back in Capernaum, Jesus resumed teaching. When he saw the huge crowds that followed him because of the miracle of the feeding of the five thousand, he admonished them to look beyond the mere fact that he had fed them with food that ultimately perishes. The food they should seek is that which leads to eternal life.

Drawing heavily on Old Testament imagery, particularly the account of the manna in the desert (Ex. 16), Jesus told his hearers of the bread from heaven that God gives to those who believe in him. Jesus himself was sent from heaven, like the manna in Moses' day, to give life to those who believe in him. That life, Jesus said, will extend beyond the grave to the resurrection.

Once again Jesus' words found great opposition from some who had come to Capernaum from Nazareth. They had known Jesus all his life. He had grown up in their midst. How could he say he was the bread of life? How could he say he had come down from heaven? They had known him since the time he was a small child, and they knew his father and mother. Jesus' response to such questions was simply to acknowledge that they did not understand him because God had not called them. They did not understand the meaning of the manna in the Old Testament or the spiritual reality it pictured.

As if to prove Jesus' point, the crowd began to ask, "How can this man give us his flesh to eat?" (John 6:52). In response, Jesus did not try to explain himself further. He, in fact, spoke all the more figuratively of himself as the bread of life: "Whoever eats my flesh and drinks my blood remains in me, and I in him" (6:56). Jesus was convinced that those whom God had called would understand the spiritual meaning of his words.

Many Disciples Offended (John 6:60–69)

After leaving the crowd at the synagogue in Capernaum, Jesus explained further to his disciples his statements about himself as the "bread of life": "The words I have spoken to you are spirit and they are life" (John 6:63). They were not meant to be taken literally. Rather, they were a picture of his coming to give life to those who believed. It would not be the mere life that physical bread gives the body; it would be eternal life. When Jesus' friends and neighbors heard him speaking of spiritual things, they could not understand him. To understand such things, Jesus said, one had to be given a new life from God; only then could one believe.

Even many of Jesus' disciples turned away from him at this time. They too had not been chosen by God and hence could not understand the spiritual dimensions of his words. The twelve apostles, however, had been chosen, and they remained with Jesus.

The Gospel accounts imply that Jesus traveled to Jerusalem to celebrate the Passover for a third time after his baptism, though there is no actual account of that journey in Scripture. That Jesus did, in fact, attend the Passover is supported by the overall pattern of his life in keeping such important feast days and by Old Testament regulations that he obeyed (see Deut. 16:16).

After the celebration, we may assume Jesus returned immediately to Galilee, presumably Capernaum, where we find him again carrying out the final stages of his ministry there. The Gospel of John tells us that Jesus remained in Galilee and purposefully stayed away from Jerusalem "because the Jews there were waiting to take his life" (John 7:1).

Discussion With Jews From Jerusalem
(Matt. 15:1–20; Mark 7:1–23)

By this time Jesus' attitude towards the religious leaders in Israel had become considerably more polemical. For the first time he engaged in a specific debate with the Pharisees over the use and meaning of the Jewish law (see Matt. 5 for his earlier comments on the law). Some Pharisees had come from Jerusalem to hear Jesus teach. They immediately noticed that some of his disciples did not keep the legal traditions as they themselves had taught. The disciples did not, for example, ceremonially cleanse their hands before eating. According to the traditions of the elders, one ought to wash one's hands carefully and wash all eating utensils such as pots, pans, and plates. The Pharisees thus asked Jesus why some of his disciples did not follow those traditions.

Jesus, apparently judging the intent of their question to be an attack on his sincerity, replied by charging the Pharisees themselves with hypocrisy and mere external traditionalism. They had used tradition to blunt the intent of the Scriptures, he contended. He cited as an example the legal custom they had devised of pronouncing a sum of money or piece of property as "Corban," that is, destined as a temple offering. In so doing, others who might have a rightful claim on that property would have to forfeit it. Consequently, parents who might claim a certain share of their children's property would thereby lose that right. Such a custom, Jesus maintained, was frequently used as an excuse to avoid giving one's own parents their fair share of one's property and thus deny them the honor and support due them according to the Scriptures.

This example of hypocrisy led to an overall warning from Jesus not to neglect purity of the heart. Mere external formalism does not treat the root cause of sin, which lies in the heart. Only God can change the heart.

The Syrophoenician Woman
(Matt. 15:22–28; Mark 7:25–30)

Jesus now traveled with his twelve apostles to several places outside the land of his countrymen. This took him first to the Mediterranean coastline, where he visited the cities of Tyre and Sidon. This was a Gentile area, the very region to which he had earlier warned his disciples not to go (Matt. 15:21; Mark 7:24).

Jesus entered a house in Tyre, hoping to remain anonymous. But even in this Gentile city, he was recognized, and word of his presence there spread quickly. A Gentile (Syrophoenician) woman came to Jesus at the house, begging him to heal her daughter, who was possessed by a demon. Jesus at first ignored her. When she persisted, Jesus told her his mission was not to the Gentiles, but to the lost sheep of Israel. The woman, however, could not so easily be dismissed. She would not take no for an answer. Jesus recognized in her persistence an evidence of true faith and healed her daughter.

Jesus then traveled eastward through Sidon, another Gentile region, returning to the area around the Sea of Galilee known as Decapolis (Mark 7:31), also a region inhabited largely by Gentiles. The Decapolis, strictly speaking, consisted of ten cities mostly situated east of the Jordan River. The term is also used to describe a wider geographical area where there were many towns and villages. We are not told in Scripture the specific parts of the Decapolis to which Jesus traveled. It was, however, an area near the Sea of Galilee.

Jesus Continues His Ministry of Healing (Matt. 15:29–39; Mark 7:32–8:10)

Once back on the shores of the Sea of Galilee, Jesus resumed his ministry of healing the sick. Many afflicted were brought to him—the lame, the blind, the crippled, the mute—and he healed them. The crowds who looked on continued to be amazed at Jesus' power over disease and affliction. They appear to have correctly concluded that Jesus had been sent by God because they praised "the God of Israel" when they saw the works he did (Matt. 15:31).

The Gospel of Mark recounts one particular example of how Jesus performed his healing miracles during this period. A deaf man with a severe speech impediment was brought to Jesus. The crowds wanted Jesus merely to lay his hands on the man and heal him. Jesus, however, took the man aside from the crowd and put his fingers into the man's ears. He then spit into his hand and touch the man's tongue with saliva. Jesus then looked into heaven and gave a deep sigh, saying, "*Ephphatha!*" (Aramaic for "Be opened!"). At that, the man's ears were opened, and he began to speak normally.

As he so often did, Jesus warned the man, and the crowd, not to spread the news of these events; but, as usual, it spread widely. The more he ordered them not to tell anyone, the faster the news spread.

For three days the crowd had followed Jesus. They had been so intent on being with him that they had not taken time out to eat. Feeling compassion on the crowd, Jesus took their remaining seven loaves of bread and a few fish and multiplied them so that four thousand men, plus the women and children, were fed that day.

Jesus then traveled by boat to the region of Dalmanutha and Magadan (located along the banks of the Sea of Galilee), probably the home of Mary Magdalene (Matt. 15:39; Mark 8:10).

Jesus Reasons With the Jews and His Own Disciples (Matt. 16:1–12; Mark 8:11–21)

Once again Jesus was visited by a delegation of Pharisees—perhaps back in Capernaum—seeking to test him and asking for a sign. They came prepared to argue, but Jesus deflected their question with an observation from everyday experience. Common sense is able to discern many signs around us. Sailors know what the weather will be at sea from the signs they see in the sky. Jesus suggested that there were many such signs in the world pointing to "the times" in which they lived, which the Pharisees understood well. If "a wicked and adulterous generation" overlooks those signs, Jesus said, they look "for a miraculous sign" (Matt. 16:4); but such signs would not be given them. The only sign they could expect to see was the "sign of Jonah," which, as we later learn, was Jesus' own resurrection.

Jesus and his disciples sailed back across the Sea of Galilee to Bethsaida. En route it was discovered that the disciples had forgotten to bring a fresh supply of bread for the journey. Jesus, characteristically, saw a spiritual lesson here. He thus warned them to beware of the yeast of the Pharisees and Sadducees. The disciples, overlooking the spiritual point, thought Jesus was scolding them for forgetting to bring enough bread. Jesus reminded the disciples of the times he multiplied the loaves of bread to feed the crowds. In other words, he was not worried about having enough bread for their journey. He was warning his disciples about the "yeast" of the Pharisees and Sadducees, that is, the "teaching" of these religious and political leaders.

Blind Man Healed at Bethsaida
and Back to Jerusalem (Mark 8:22-26; John 7:1-9)

When Jesus and his disciples arrived at Bethsaida, a blind man was brought to him. Those who brought the man to Jesus wanted only that he touch the man and heal him. Jesus, however, did more than that. First, he took the man by the hand and led him out of the village. He then spit on the man's eyes, laid his hands on him, and asked the man whether he could see. The man said he could see but not clearly—people looked like trees walking about. Jesus then laid his hands on the man again, and the man began to see clearly.

When the time of the Jewish Feast of Tabernacles arrived, Jesus' brothers challenged him to go openly to the feast and show himself to the world as the Messiah. In his response to them, Jesus revealed that he was working according to a long-established divine plan. He was waiting for the right time to come, the time established by his heavenly Father and known only to him. Jesus was speaking of the time of the Passover, which would come in that same year. At that feast he would ride triumphantly into Jerusalem to claim the kingdom and the throne of David. At present, Jesus was satisfied to go to the Feast of Tabernacles alone and secretly.

Jesus at the Feast of Tabernacles (John 7:10–53)

When Jesus arrived at the Feast of Tabernacles, he found a good deal of discussion about him. Everyone seemed to have an opinion. Some said he was a good man; others, that he was a deceiver. All were afraid to discuss him openly, however, because they were afraid of the religious leaders, who by this time vehemently opposed Jesus.

Midway through the feast, Jesus went into the temple court and began to teach. The crowds who had come to celebrate the feast were amazed at his teaching. How could he have such wisdom without a formal education? Jesus' answer was that he had received his education from God, the One who had sent him.

The fact that Jesus had come to the feast and was teaching openly at the temple raised an important question in the mind of the crowds. Was Jesus not the one whom the religious leaders were seeking to put to death? Why then was he allowed to teach openly at the temple? Did this perhaps mean that the authorities now believed him to be the Messiah? The crowd raised another question: How could this man, Jesus, whom they all knew to be from the little town of Nazareth, be the Messiah? The irony of their question was brought out clearly in Jesus' reply. While it was true that he was born in Nazareth, it was not true that they knew where he was "from." Jesus was from eternity (John 1:1); he was sent from God (7:29).

Such claims by Jesus aroused a great deal of animosity among many in the crowd. They rushed at him to seize him, but he escaped their grasp. Still others in the crowd understood Jesus' point and believed in him. When the authorities called on the temple guards to arrest Jesus, he again eluded them.

On the last day of the feast, Jesus was back teaching openly in the temple. The crowds who listened were also openly divided. A central issue was the fact that Jesus had come to Jerusalem from Galilee, whereas the people were looking for the Messiah to come from Bethlehem, the city of David. The fact that Jesus had, in fact, been born in Bethlehem and was of the house of David was, apparently at that time, not widely known by the crowds.

When the temple guards were called and asked why they had not arrested Jesus, they acknowledged that they themselves were amazed at him. The religious authorities who had called out the guards were now perplexed. Had even the leaders of the Pharisees begun to believe Jesus? The guards answered emphatically, "No!" There were no religious leaders who believed in Jesus, they maintained.

At that, Nicodemus, a secret believer and an important religious leader, took the occasion to rescue Jesus from their plot to kill him. In doing so he came close to tipping his own hand about Jesus. Fortunately, the rulers, not suspecting that Nicodemus could possibly be a believer, resorted to sarcasm: "Are you from Galilee, too?" as if to imply that in speaking up for Jesus he was merely rooting for his own hometown of Galilee. Nicodemus, therefore, did not have to answer the self-incriminating question: "Do you also believe in Jesus?"

Further Teaching at the Temple (John 7:53–8:59)

Jesus left the temple courtyard and spent the night on the Mount of Olives. At dawn the next day he was again at the temple. Large crowds had gathered around him, and he taught them. In order to trap Jesus in a legal opinion, the religious authorities brought a woman convicted of adultery to Jesus and asked what her sentence should be. At first, Jesus appeared to ignore their question. He merely looked down and wrote with his finger on the ground. But they kept up with their question. So he replied, "If any one of you is without sin, let him be the first to throw a stone at her" (John 8:7). At that, he began writing on the ground again. One by one, the questioners began to walk away, the oldest first. After everyone had left and Jesus was alone with the woman, he turned to her and admonished her, "Go now and leave your life of sin."

Jesus continued to speak to the people who had come to the temple. As he taught, the Pharisees asked him many questions, challenging the validity of his teaching. By what authority could he claim its truthfulness? Jesus responded by claiming the authority of God, who had sent him, and that of the Scriptures. Though he was openly opposed by the religious authorities at the temple, he continued to teach unmolested.

In the end, however, his teaching was too controversial even for many in the crowd. They understood him to be saying that he had known their ancestor Abraham and that Abraham had known him. Jesus replied, "Before Abraham was born, I am!" Immediately recognizing the implication of Jesus' answer, many picked up stones and were intent on killing him. Jesus, however, slipped away from the temple grounds to safety.

Jesus Heals a Man Born Blind
(John 9:1–10:21)

As Jesus walked through the streets of Jerusalem, he saw a blind man begging by the side of the road. The disciples asked Jesus what they thought to be a serious theological question: "Rabbi, who sinned, this man or his parents, that he was born blind?" Jesus' answer lay deeper than either of these alternatives. This man was born blind, he said, in order to show the work of God in his life. To show what he meant by this, Jesus spit on the ground and mixed a small bit of mud from his saliva and placed it on the man's eyes. He then told the man to wash himself in a nearby pool in Jerusalem, the Pool of Siloam. The man had been born blind, Jesus implied, to demonstrate God's power in Jerusalem. Jesus looked beyond the immediate causes of the events to the ultimate plan and purposes of God.

When the man had washed himself in the Pool of Siloam, he received sight. His neighbors, who had known him all his life, recognized him and were amazed that he could now see. They wanted to know who had healed him. They also brought the man to the Pharisees.

The Pharisees concluded that Jesus could not have been sent to do the work of God because he performed this miracle on the Sabbath. Others, presumably those that brought the man to the Pharisees, were not satisfied with that answer. No one could deny that Jesus had performed a miracle, but a sinner certainly could not do such wondrous signs.

Next the Pharisees turned to the man who had been healed. Who did he think the man was? The man spoke with uncanny clarity. "He is a prophet," he said. Some in the crowd were still not convinced. How did they know the man had really been blind? They thus sought the man's parents to ensure this fact. The parents, while willing to say both that this was their son and that he had been born blind, were unwilling to say how he had now gained his sight. Their son was of age, they argued, so he should speak for himself. They were unwilling to speak up for Jesus for fear of being cast out of the synagogue.

The former blind man, however, viewed things differently. How else could Jesus' works be explained? God does not answer the prayers of sinners, yet he had certainly done this great deed. Jesus must have been sent from God! The religious authorities were unwilling to accept the word of this man. His blindness was itself a sign to them that he was a sinner. Because he spoke favorably about Jesus, they threw him out of the synagogue.

The actions of the Pharisees and their unwillingness to see the hand of God in the miraculous healing of the blind man were a sign to Jesus of their own sinfulness. They, not the blind man, were the ones born in sin. They were the ones who were truly blind, because they were unwilling to see. The blind man could hear Jesus before he could see him; the Pharisees could see Jesus but refused to hear what he had to say. Jesus was the "good shepherd," who would lay down his life for his sheep. Like the blind man, his sheep were those who heard his voice and followed him (John 10).

Peter's Confession and Jesus' Coming Suffering (Matt. 16:13-23; Mark 8:27-33; Luke 9:18-22; John 6:67-71)

A great division of opinion about Jesus broke out among those who were listening to him. Some rejected Jesus altogether and refused to listen to him further. Others were not satisfied with the view that Jesus was not from God, and they were willing to listen further. On that note Jesus left Jerusalem and returned to Galilee. Taking his disciples, he went to Caesarea Philippi (Mark 8:27). It was there that Peter's own eyes began to open. He was the first among the disciples who began to understand who Jesus really was.

During their journey to Caesarea Philippi, Jesus focused his disciples' attention on his true identity. He began with the question of what the crowds thought about Jesus: "Who do people say the Son of Man is?" (Matt. 16:13). His disciples answered Jesus with a litany of possibilities— John the Baptist, Elijah, Jeremiah, or one of the other prophets. Then Jesus asked the more immediate question: "But who do you say I am?" Peter answered for the whole group: "You are the Christ, the Son of the living God." Peter's answer, Jesus said, could only have come from the Father. That answer was, in fact, to be the cornerstone of the church that God was going to found by means of the work of these apostles.

Jesus warned his disciples not to spread the word that he was the Messiah (the Christ). God, in his own timing, would make that known to the world. Jesus was fully aware of what awaited him on his next journey to Jerusalem. He, in fact, was careful to give his disciples a full account of what would happen to him as Messiah. He would "suffer many things at the hands of the elders, chief priests and teachers of the law, and . . . be killed and on the third day be raised to life" (Matt. 16:21).

Hearing such words, Peter objected vehemently to them: "Never, Lord!" he maintained. "This shall never happen to you!" (Matt. 16:22).

Though Peter thought he was expressing God's will, Jesus sternly warned him that such thoughts were in direct opposition to that will (Matt. 16:23). After all, Jesus had been sent by the Father for one purpose: to give his life to establish the long-awaited messianic kingdom (Matt. 16:24–28), and that required the way of the cross. Nothing could, or should, stand in the way of that goal.

The Transfiguration
(Matt. 17:1–9; Mark 9:2–10; Luke 9:28–36)

Jesus had told his disciples that some of them would not see death until they saw him coming in his kingdom. Jesus was probably referring here to his "transfiguration" appearance. Six days later, Jesus took three of the disciples, Peter, James, and John, to a high mountain in Galilee to pray. There he revealed to them a vision of the glory of the future kingdom.

As they prayed, Jesus began to be "transfigured" before their eyes—he took upon himself the glorious appearance he will have when he establishes the kingdom of God in the future. His face shone like the sun, and his clothes were dazzling white. They also saw Moses and Elijah talking with Jesus about what would soon happen to him in Jerusalem. Then a cloud surrounded and enveloped them. God's voice came out of the cloud, saying, "This is my Son, whom I love."

The disciples were terrified at what they saw. They fell face down on the ground. Then they heard the voice of Jesus, and when they looked up, they saw him standing with them alone. He sternly warned the three to tell no one what they had seen until after the resurrection.

The sight of Elijah and Moses speaking with Jesus prompted the three disciples to ask about Elijah's coming to prepare the way for the Messiah. Jesus replied that Elijah had, in fact, already come and had been rejected—just as Jesus, the Messiah, had come and was being rejected. The disciples understood Jesus to be speaking about John the Baptist.

In this event, Peter, James, and John were given not only a preview of the glory of the coming kingdom of God, but also an explanation of why there would be a delay before the establishment of that kingdom. Both John and Jesus had been rejected by the people of God in their own day, but God's promises would remain firm. A time was yet to come when Jesus would return and rule in his kingdom.

Healings and Discussions
(Matt. 17:14–18:35; Mark 9:14–50; Luke 9:37–50)

While Jesus was on the mountain in Galilee praying, a man brought his demon-possessed son to the disciples. In Jesus' absence, the disciples were unable to heal him. The religious leaders seized on the disciples' failure and argued strenuously with them. When the man brought his son to Jesus after he returned, Jesus healed him.

The disciples were puzzled that they had been unable to heal the boy. When they approached Jesus with their concern, he told them it was because of their little faith. They had been given authority to drive demons out, (Matt. 10:1), but they had to have faith to exercise that authority. If they did, Jesus said, they could even move mountains.

Jesus left the area of the Mount of Transfiguration and traveled toward Capernaum. En route he reminded his disciples of what he had told them earlier (Matt. 16:21)—that he would be betrayed, killed, and rise from the grave on the third day. The disciples were greatly saddened by these words, though they did not understand what he was saying and were afraid to ask him.

When Jesus arrived at Capernaum (Matt. 17:24; Mark 9:33), the temple tax collector approached Peter, seeking the annual tax for the upkeep of the temple (cf. Ex. 30:13—two drachmas per person). Jesus believed himself to be exempt from such taxes, but he was intent on paying his share so as not to offend the religious authorities. Jesus thus told Peter to go out to the lake and cast his line into the water. He would find the needed money for his and Jesus' tax (i.e., four drachmas) in the mouth of the first fish he caught.

The disciples came to Jesus with a question of who would be the greatest in the kingdom of heaven. Jesus answered by calling a small child over to him. The greatest in the kingdom, he said, was one like this humble, trusting child. Jesus went on to teach the disciples many things about humility, concern for others, forgiveness, correcting others' faults, and showing mercy.

Jesus' Last Trip to Jerusalem

Departure From Galilee and the Sending of the Seventy-Two
(Matt. 19:1; Mark 10:1; Luke 9:51–10:24)

The time had come for Jesus to go up to Jerusalem to present himself to the nation as their Messiah. Matthew tells us that "when Jesus had finished saying these things, he left Galilee" (Matt. 19:1). The Gospel of Luke saw this as the time when Jesus was about to be "taken up to heaven" (Luke 9:51).

Many things happened to Jesus and his disciples on the way to Jerusalem. A major part of each of the four Gospels, especially Luke (see 9:51–19:28), is devoted to the events leading up to the last week in the ministry of Jesus. Nearly half of the Gospel of Mark is devoted to the actual events of that final week in Jerusalem.

In preparation for his journey, Jesus sent messengers ahead to reserve lodging in a Samaritan village. Knowing that he was heading for Jerusalem, the Samaritans were unwilling to accommodate him. Jesus' disciples took great offense at that treatment. James and John were ready to call down fire from heaven upon the city. Jesus, however, rebuked the two brothers and turned away to another village.

Jesus also at the time chose seventy-two of his followers and sent them in groups of two into every town and village he was about to enter. They were to be "workers in the harvest fields"—to heal the sick and announce that the kingdom of God was near. They were to stay in the houses of those who received their words. If any town or household refused to welcome them or rejected their words, they were to leave that place and go on to another.

Days or perhaps a week later, the seventy-two returned to report to Jesus on the success of their mission. They returned with great joy at what they had experienced. Jesus saw their mission as a great defeat of Satan. Many persons had been won for the kingdom of God by their witness. Jesus saw this as the beginning of the fulfillment of what the Old Testament prophets had long ago envisioned for Israel. The messianic kingdom was beginning to take shape among God's people.

A Lawyer's Question and the Lord's Prayer
(Luke 10:25–37; 11:1–13)

In one of the towns Jesus visited on his trip to Jerusalem, he was met by an authority on the Jewish law. His discussion with Jesus centered on what the law had to say about eternal life. The law, Jesus replied, requires love of God and love of one's neighbor. But, the man asked Jesus, "Who is my neighbor?" In answer to that question, Jesus told the story of the good Samaritan. The point of the story was clear: One's neighbor is anyone in need of mercy and compassion.

Throughout his ministry, Jesus prayed regularly and at great length. Now, as he approached the final stages of his ministry, one of his disciples asked him to teach them to pray. Jesus responded by giving them a brief model prayer, one he had already taught them early on in his ministry: the Lord's Prayer (see Matt. 6:9–13).

In addition to this model prayer, Jesus also taught his disciples the importance of incessant and persistent prayer. God is like a loving father who gives his children the good things they ask him for.

A Day in the Life of Jesus En Route to Jerusalem (Luke 11:14–13:9)

The Gospel of Luke gives us a fairly complete picture of a day in the life of Jesus during his final journey to Jerusalem. His day began with casting a demon out of a mute man. When the man began to speak, the crowd was greatly amazed. Some, however, questioned the authority by which Jesus performed such miracles. Others wanted to see a sign from heaven to verify his authority. Jesus responded to their accusations as he had done on earlier occasions (Matt. 12:25–28): If one cast out demons, he must surely do so by God's authority.

Hearing Jesus' words, a woman cried out from the crowd, "Blessed is the mother who gave you birth and nursed you." Jesus replied, "Blessed rather are those who hear the word of God and obey it."

As Jesus looked around him and saw that the crowd was increasing in size, he began to warn them about the coming days of judgment. He compared them to the people of Nineveh, who repented when they saw the sign of Jonah's rescue by the great fish. His own resurrection, Jesus asserted, would be just such a sign for this generation. The difference was that they, unlike Nineveh, would not repent. Nor would they be like the Queen of Sheba (1 Kings 10:1), who came from the ends of the earth to hear Solomon's wisdom. Even though one much greater in wisdom and power than Solomon was now in their midst, this generation had no interest in him. Their hearts were full of darkness.

When Jesus had finished teaching the crowd, he was invited into the home of a Pharisee. The Pharisee, however, took offense at Jesus' failure to cleanse himself ceremonially before the meal. Jesus replied that washing the body did not affect the heart. Cleansing the heart with acts of justice and love of God was far more important than ceremonially washing the body.

Some of those present accused Jesus of speaking against the Jewish law. Jesus, however, turned the tables on them. It was not he who insulted the law; rather, it was the legal experts who neglected the teachings of Scripture and added countless burdensome details to the law. In doing so, the religious authorities in his day were like their own forefathers, who persecuted and killed the prophets (Luke 11:47). The legal experts held the key to the Scriptures, but they used it to lock up those Scriptures so that neither they nor the people they taught could understand them.

Jesus' words greatly troubled the Pharisees and teachers of the law. They followed him and "began to oppose him fiercely and to besiege him with questions, waiting to catch him in something he might say" (Luke 11:53–54). As the crowds grew into the thousands, Jesus continued to warn them about the hypocrisy of their religious leaders. Purity of heart is far more important than actions designed only to appease the authorities. God knows the heart, and he will one day judge all according their standing firm in the teaching they had heard from Jesus.

Someone in the crowd then asked Jesus to make a judgment in a legal matter he had with his brother over their inheritance. Jesus flatly refused, warning the man of the greed that lay behind such matters. He then illustrated his point with a parable of the wealthy fool, who put all his trust in material possessions but neglected his walk with God (Luke 12:16–21). God will take care of his own; there is no need for worry. Be ready and faithful in his work. Though there may be a delay in establishing God's kingdom, its time will come, and we must be ready and wait for it. Hard times await the faithful in the future. We must be alert and able to interpret the times.

While Jesus was speaking, news arrived that the Roman governor, Pontius Pilate, had slain some Galilean Jews while they were offering sacrifices at the temple. Such events, Jesus asserted, were not brought on by the individual guilt of the victims. They show the reality that faces all human beings—everyone will perish some day. The call to repent is imperative.

Healing the Crippled Woman on the Sabbath (Luke 13:10–30)

On another occasion, Jesus was teaching in one of the synagogues on the Sabbath. He saw in the crowd a woman who had been crippled for eighteen years. She was bound by an evil spirit. Calling the woman forward, Jesus healed her and praised God. The ruler of the synagogue, however, was greatly incensed that Jesus would do such a thing on the Sabbath. Wasn't there plenty of time during the week for such things? Jesus, however, responded by calling the ruler's concern an instance of hypocrisy. Some things are good to do anytime during the week. Doesn't everyone lead their donkey to water, even on the Sabbath? How much more ought one to heal this woman on the Sabbath!

Jesus' reply humiliated his opponents, but the crowd was overjoyed at seeing the woman healed. Taking this occasion, Jesus continued to teach the crowd in parables about the kingdom of God.

While traveling through the towns and villages on his way to Jerusalem, Jesus was asked whether only a few would be saved. The way was narrow, he replied. Many would be surprised that they have been excluded from the kingdom. Many others would take the place of the rightful heirs of the kingdom.

Warnings, Lament, and a Visit to Bethany (Luke 10:38–42; 13:31–35)

As Jesus was continuing on to Jerusalem, some Pharisees came to him to warn him that Herod planned to kill him. Jesus, however, was unmoved. It was appointed for him to die in Jerusalem, he told the Pharisees—just as it had been appointed for the other prophets before him.

Jesus was deeply grieved over Jerusalem's rejection of him and his kingdom. He had come to gather them as a hen gathers her chicks, but they were unwilling to come to him. The day would come, Jesus promised, when he would come again to his people, and they would recognize him as their blessed Redeemer who comes in the name of the Lord.

By now Jesus was nearing Bethany, west of the Jordan River and just east of Jerusalem, where he planned to stay at the home of Mary and Martha. While there, Mary showed a deep interest in Jesus' teaching. Leaving the work of caring for Jesus to her sister, she sat at Jesus' feet listening to his every word. Seeing that her sister was neglecting her duties, Martha complained to Jesus. Jesus, however, praised the single-minded devotion of Mary. Her focus was on eternal things, while Martha's was on only things of immediate concern.

In Jerusalem and to Perea (John 10:22–42)

It was now winter, and the time for Hanukkah (Feast of Dedication) had come. Jesus thus entered Jerusalem and went to the temple. As he walked through the area of the outer court called Solomon's Porch, a crowd began to gather around him. Some Jews confronted Jesus, wanting to hear from him whether he claimed to be the Messiah. Jesus responded that the miraculous works he had done among them were plain enough evidence of who he was. If they did not believe, it was only because the heavenly Father had not called them and given them the faith to believe. Jesus concluded his answer with the claim, "I and the Father are one" (John 10:30). At that, many picked up stones and were intent on killing him. How could a mere man claim to be God?

Jesus, in his own defense, reminded the crowd that the Old Testament Scriptures speak of human instruments of God as "gods" (Ps. 82:6). Why then cannot the Chosen One, the Messiah, also be called "God"? It was certainly not blasphemy, Jesus continued, to refer to oneself as the "Son of God." Jesus' words, however, fell on deaf ears. The crowd was intent on seizing Jesus, but he escaped their grasp.

At the end of the Feast of Dedication Jesus withdrew from Jerusalem and traveled back across the Jordan River, where John had baptized many in preparation for the coming kingdom of God (John 1:28). This was a region known in ancient times as Perea. During the time from Hanukkah to Passover (about four months), Jesus appears to have spent much of this time in this area, though he occasionally traveled to Bethany as well (cf. Luke 14:1–17:10). Many people of Perea came out to see Jesus; they testified that all John the Baptist had said about Jesus was true. Also many from the region around Bethany believed in Jesus at this time.

At a Pharisee's House (Luke 14:1–15:32)

Jesus was in the home of an important, and probably high-ranking, Pharisee on the Sabbath day. By now he was being carefully watched to see if he could be caught violating any Jewish laws. A man appeared before him suffering from dropsy. Before healing him, Jesus raised the inevitable question of whether it was lawful to heal on the Sabbath. Those present refused to answer. Jesus healed the man and sent him away. If one could rescue a son or an ox on the Sabbath, he reasoned, it was surely proper to heal a diseased man on the Sabbath.

Seeing the guests arrayed around the table at the Pharisee's house, Jesus was prompted to speak about the importance of genuine humility. Some had taken seats of honor, while others had deferred to them and taken the lesser seats. Assuming a place of honor can backfire into disgrace, Jesus warned his company. True acts of humility and grace will find their reward at the time of judgment after the resurrection. Many religious people will be caught up short in that day because they have not answered Jesus' call to come into the kingdom.

After Jesus left the house, he continued to travel throughout the region west of the Jordan River, teaching the crowd in parables. Much of what he taught stressed discipleship and faithfulness to his mission (Luke 14:25–35). Many who followed him were not a part of the religious establishment; they were "tax collectors and 'sinners.'" Such a following aroused suspicion and jealousy among the religious elite (15:1–2). But Jesus used such situations to teach the need to seek out and save the lost and dejected of this world. During this time he taught three of his most memorable parables: the lost sheep (15:3–7), the lost coin (15:8–10), and the prodigal (lost) son (15:11–32).

The Old Testament and the Kingdom (Luke 16:1–17:10)

Jesus also taught his chosen disciples during this time on the importance of the Old Testament Scriptures. Jesus was soon going to leave them; they would have only the Scriptures and the Spirit to guide them.

On many occasions, the Pharisees listened in on his teaching. When, on one occasion, Jesus taught his disciples the parable of the shrewd manager (Luke 16:1–13), the Pharisees began to ridicule Jesus for his teaching. Jesus taught that money and wealth were of value only as a means for doing good and thus securing an eternal reward. The Pharisees, who loved money for its own sake, thought this to be a great folly (16:14–15).

In response to the attitude of the Pharisees, Jesus pointed to the fact that the Scriptures teach that God does not look upon those things that impress and dazzle human beings, such as money, wealth, power, and prestige. God looks at the heart. Moreover, Jesus went on, the Old Testament Scriptures also looked forward to the time when God's kingdom would rule among human beings on this earth. When John came preaching in the desert, he was announcing the good news of the coming of that kingdom (Luke 16:16). Not a single Old Testament promise about that kingdom would fail to come about. It was, in fact, being fulfilled before their own eyes (16:17). Its fulfillment meant that not only the external acts of righteousness were essential to godly living, but also the purity of one's inward attitude.

At this time, some Pharisees engaged Jesus in a discussion about the application of the Law of Moses to life. What about divorce? "Is it lawful for a man to divorce his wife for any and every reason?" (Matt. 19:3). Jesus replied to the question from the Scriptures. In the Old Testament narratives, he said, marriage is treated as a divinely ordained institution. At marriage, the man and woman are "no longer two, but one" (19:6). They cannot, and should not, be separated. The Pharisees responded with their own argument from the Old Testament law: Did not Moses, in the Law, allow for a "certificate of divorce" (19:7)? Yes, said Jesus, Moses permitted divorce because the hearts of the people were not capable of fulfilling the requirements of God's will. God gave them an exception, but his will always was and is that a married couple remain one (Matt. 19:8–9; Luke 16:18).

Jesus continued to teach his disciples about the importance of Scripture. In a few weeks they were going to witness his resurrection, which would have a fundamental effect on their lives. It would not, however, stand as their central foundation in their continuing to follow Jesus; that would be the Scriptures. To make this point, Jesus taught his disciples the parable of the rich man and Lazarus (Luke 16:19–31), showing that miraculous wonders, such as a resurrection, could not produce faith and open the eyes of the spiritually blind. Only the Scriptures could do that. As Abraham said to the rich man in this parable, "If they do not listen to Moses and the Prophets [Scripture], they will not be convinced even if someone rises from the dead" (Luke 16:31). As he did on many occasions, Jesus concluded his teaching with a call for repentance, faith, and perseverance (Luke 17:1–10).

The Illness, Death, and Resurrection of Lazarus (John 11:1-44)

While Jesus was teaching in Perea, he received word that his good friend Lazarus, the brother of Mary and Martha, was sick. After waiting two days, Jesus left Perea, crossed the Jordan, and reentered Judea. His disciples warned him that this was dangerous territory in which to travel. Only a short time before, the religious authorities had tried to stone him. Jesus was, however, clearly aware of the danger and passed through the region unharmed. By now he knew that Lazarus had died, so he made his way to Bethany, intent on raising him from the dead.

When Jesus arrived at the edge of the city, he was told that Larazus had been dead for four days. Many from Jerusalem had arrived to mourn his death. Hearing that Jesus was at the edge of town, Martha went out to meet him. Jesus told her that he would raise Lazarus if she would only believe in him. Martha replied with the confession, "I believe that you are the Christ [Messiah], the Son of God, who was to come into the world" (John 11:27). Such a confession shows a remarkable understanding on her part of who Jesus was, even before the resurrection.

Martha returned to her sister, who had remained at home. Mary went quickly to Jesus too. Those in her house followed her, thinking she was going to the grave of Lazarus. Seeing Mary and the crowd of mourners following her, Jesus asked to be taken to the tomb. Jesus wept on the way. Many in the crowd wondered why Jesus had not come earlier to heal Lazarus.

When they arrived at the tomb, Jesus asked that the stone sealing the entrance of the tomb be removed. After some hesitation, Martha obeyed. Jesus said a short prayer and then called to Lazarus inside the tomb. Lazarus came out, still wrapped in his burial clothes. Seeing Lazarus, many in the crowd believed in Jesus. Some, however, reported the event to the Pharisees.

The Plot to Arrest and Kill Jesus (John 11:45–57)

Having heard that Jesus had raised Lazarus from the dead, the religious leaders in Jerusalem called a special session of the Sanhedrin, the highest governing body within ancient Judaism. It consisted of members of the Sadducees, the Pharisees, and the priests, and members of households and representatives of the people. The Sanhedrin conceded that Jesus had performed miracles and that the crowds believed he was the Messiah. They feared that the Romans would use his popularity as an excuse to crush their nation and dissolve their own rule.

In the midst of the discussion, the high priest, Caiaphas, rose to address the assembly. Unwittingly, he prophesied to the assembly about the impending death of Jesus. Its purpose, he said, was that one man should die to save the nation. The response of the Sanhedrin to these words was to initiate a plan to kill Jesus.

Jesus, therefore, withdrew from public view. He made his way to a village called Ephraim, near the desert region of Judea, where he stayed with his disciples, privately and away from the crowds. The time was approaching, however, when he would make himself known publicly in Jerusalem.

As the time for the Passover drew near, many traveling to Jerusalem to prepare for that festival kept looking for Jesus and wondered whether he would be coming. It was widely known that the religious leaders had put a price on his head.

The Grateful Leper and a Question About the Kingdom (Luke 17:11–18:14)

Jesus fully intended to celebrate the Feast of Passover in Jerusalem. At the appropriate time, he left the little village of Ephraim and entered a village near Samaria, where he was met by a group of ten lepers. Nine of them were Jews; the other was a Samaritan. Standing at a distance, they called out to Jesus for mercy and healing. Telling them to show themselves to the priests, Jesus healed them. Only one of the ten—the Samaritan—returned to thank Jesus.

As he traveled openly toward Jerusalem, a Pharisee asked Jesus when the kingdom of God would be established. Jesus answered his question by pointing out that the kingdom was already in their midst but they did not recognize it. He was the King.

Jesus then turned to teach his disciples about the future establishment of the kingdom of God as prophesied throughout the Old Testament Scriptures. Jesus was the "Son of Man" of whom Daniel the prophet spoke. He would one day establish the long-awaited kingdom. In the meanwhile, however, he would be rejected. Life would go on as usual for some time before it was established. It would be like the days of Noah, when God waited many years before sending the Flood, and like the days before Sodom was destroyed. When the kingdom did come, however, it would come swiftly and terribly for those not expecting it.

Jesus concluded his discourse on the kingdom with two parables, the unjust judge (Luke 18:1–8) and the Pharisee and the tax collector (Luke 18:9–14). Both parables stressed the importance of faithful and humble persistence in faith. Jesus was preparing his disciples for what lay ahead for them. They would have to wait for the final coming of his kingdom.

Further Events on the Way to Jerusalem
(Matt. 19:13–20:19; Mark 10:13–34; Luke 18:15–34)

While continuing on to Jerusalem, Jesus was met by many who brought babies to him. The disciples were offended and scolded the parents. Jesus, however, was gracious to the little children. He saw their simplicity and sincerity as the primary characteristics of the kingdom of God. He took the children in his arms and blessed them.

Next a wealthy ruler approached Jesus and asked what he had to do to gain eternal life. Jesus told him to keep the commandments (which the man claimed to be doing) and to sell all his possessions, give the money to the poor, and follow Jesus. The man was greatly troubled by Jesus' words, for he found it difficult to accept the thought of giving his wealth away. Even those listening found these words hard to accept. Salvation, as Jesus understood it, was indeed hard to obtain. It was, in fact, impossible; it could only be accomplished by a gracious God.

Then Jesus took the disciples aside and explained to them why he was going to Jerusalem—to celebrate the Feast of Passover, of course, but also to fulfill everything spoken of by the Old Testament prophets. He would be condemned to death, mocked by the Gentiles, and be crucified, and on the third day he would rise from the dead. In other words, he was going to Jerusalem to give his life as the messianic Son of Man.

As a way of giving his disciples insight into how they were to carry on while waiting for Jesus to establish his kingdom, he continued to teach them through parables. In the parable of the vineyard workers Jesus taught his disciples that "the last will be first, and the first will be last" (Matt. 20:16; cf. 20:20–28; Mark 10:35–45). Jesus was, by this time, in the final stage of his journey to Jerusalem

At Jericho (Matt. 20:29–34;
Mark 10:46–52; Luke 18:35–19:10)

Jesus passed through the city of Jericho on his way to Jerusalem. At the gate of the city he was met by two blind beggars. One, named Bartimaeus, called out to Jesus for healing. His persistent cries for help caught the attention of Jesus, and he called for Bartimaeus to come near. When Jesus saw his faith, he healed both blind men.

While going through Jericho, Jesus met one of the chief tax collectors of the city. He was a wealthy man named Zacchaeus, who desperately wanted to see Jesus. He was too short, however, even to get a glimpse of Jesus over the heads of the large crowd that had gathered. Therefore, he climbed a tree along the road where Jesus was walking. When Jesus came to the foot of the tree and looked up and saw Zacchaeus, he asked him to come down so that he might stay at his house. Zacchaeus came down from the tree at once and welcomed Jesus into his home.

When the people of the city of Jericho saw that Jesus had gone into the home of a tax collector, they were scandalized. How could a godly man have fellowship with such a sinner, they wondered. Since tax collectors worked for the Romans, they were regarded with reproach by the people. Zacchaeus, however, proved to be anything but a sinner. He vowed to give half of his entire estate to the poor and to repay four times over what he had cheated from anyone. Jesus, clearly pleased with Zacchaeus's actions, acknowledged that his actions were proof that this lost man was now saved.

Parable of the Ten Minas (Luke 19:11–27)

When the people of Jericho saw what had happened to Zacchaeus and as they listened to Jesus' teaching, they began to think that the kingdom of God was, indeed, about to appear. Jesus then taught them about the kingdom in the parable of the ten minas. This parable was a not-too-subtle allusion to the events that lay just ahead in Jerusalem. In it, Jesus spoke about a man of noble birth who went to a distant country to be made king. Before leaving, he gave each of his ten servants one mina (piece of coin) to live on.

While he was gone, the nobleman was made king, and some of his subjects rebelled against him and rejected him as their king. The king then returned to see what each of his servants had done with their mina. Some had invested it and showed a good return. One, however, had merely hidden it away and had nothing to show for it. The wise servants who had invested their minas were rewarded for their faithfulness. The servant who hid his mina and did not use it was punished; his mina was taken from him and given to the servant who had gained the most. The king then punished those of his subjects who had rebelled against him.

In this parable, Jesus appears to have anticipated that the kingdom he was to establish at Jerusalem would be rejected. He would be away for a period of time, and his servants would carry on for him in his absence. Those who invested themselves in his work would be rewarded when he returned, whereas those who did not would lose even what they had been given. The rebellious subjects who rejected their king would also be punished. When he finished speaking this parable, Jesus parted from the crowds and left the city of Jericho.

Jesus Visits Bethany
(Matt. 26:6–13; Mark 14:3–9; Luke 19:28–29; John 12:1–11)

Six days before the Feast of Passover began, Jesus entered Bethany again—the village where Lazarus had been raised from the dead. Jesus was invited to dine at the home of a man known as Simon the Leper. Lazarus was present there, and Martha, his sister, served. During the meal, the other sister, Mary, came to Jesus with a pint of expensive perfume to wash Jesus' feet. Seeing what was happening, Judas, the disciple in charge of their finances, objected strongly to the use of such expensive perfume. *Shouldn't the perfume be sold and the money be given to the poor?* he thought. Jesus, however, defended Mary. This perfume was to be saved for his own coming burial.

While this was taking place inside the house, a large crowd began to gather outside. They wanted to see both Jesus and Lazarus. Many people in the village had come to believe in Jesus because of the miracle of Lazarus. The religious leaders, however, feared Jesus, and so they made plans also to kill Lazarus.

Jesus' Final Week in Jerusalem

The Triumphal Entry
(Matt. 21:1–17; Mark 11:1–11; Luke 19:29–44; John 12:12–19)

Nearing Jerusalem, Jesus came to Bethphage on the Mount of Olives. Waiting there, he sent two disciples ahead to secure a donkey for him to ride into Jerusalem. When they brought it back to Jesus, he mounted it and rode into Jerusalem. In ancient times such an act would have been understood as a royal procession; in Jesus' day it appears to have been largely symbolic, but the meaning was not lost on the large crowd of onlookers, some of whom cast their cloaks and palm branches on the road before him. A large crowd also ran ahead of him shouting, "Hosanna [Save us] to the Son of David!"

Looking out over the city from the Mount of Olives, Jesus wept as he thought about what lay ahead for the city and its people. They would soon reject him as their king, and their enemies, the Romans, would raze the city to the ground—all because they had rejected their king.

When Jesus entered the city, there was much commotion. People asked, "Who is this?" and others responded, "This is Jesus, the prophet from Nazareth in Galilee." Some Pharisees in the crowd admonished Jesus to quiet his followers, but he refused.

Once in Jerusalem itself, Jesus made his way to the temple. There many blind and lame came to him to be healed. As he walked through the temple area, little children followed him shouting, "Hosanna to the Son of David!" He remained at the temple for some time, but as it grew late, he left to spend the night in Bethany—presumably at the house of Lazarus.

Jesus' Return to the Temple
(Matt. 21:18-22:40; Mark 11:12-12:34;
Luke 19:45-20:40)

Early in the morning of the next day, Jesus left Bethany and returned to the temple. On his way he eyed a fig tree that had no fruit on it. Jesus saw the fruitless tree as a symbol of many in his own day. Speaking to the tree, Jesus said, "May you never bear fruit again!" (Matt. 21:19). As he spoke, the tree began to wither. By the next day it had completely died (Mark 11:20).

Jesus and his disciples continued toward the temple. When they arrived, he noticed much buying and selling of merchandise. As he had done at the beginning of his ministry, he drove the merchants out of the temple, overturning the tables of the money changers and those selling sacrificial doves. Moreover, he would not allow anyone even to carry merchandise through the temple courts. Such action greatly incensed the religious leaders, the chief priests, and the teachers of the law. But because Jesus was well liked by the people, these leaders dared not harm him publicly. They continued secretly, however, to draw up plans to have Jesus removed.

The religious leaders continued to question Jesus' authority, but Jesus had a ready answer to their questions. He also taught those present at the temple in parables—the central thrust of which focused on his rejection and impending death. In the parable of the tenants (Matt. 21:33-44; Mark 12:1-11; Luke 20:9-16), for example, Jesus spoke of a vineyard whose owner had gone away for a time and left the vineyard to farmers. The farmers, however, usurped the vineyard for themselves and would not share its produce with the owner. When the owner sent representatives to collect his share of the produce, like the prophets of old, they were beaten and killed. Finally, the owner sent his own son, but the farmers killed him as well. Thereupon, the owner returned and cast the farmers out of the vineyard and then gave it to others.

Such parables were thinly disguised indictments against the religious leaders of Jesus' own day, who had taken the promises of God to Israel and usurped them for their own glory. Jesus contended that they beat and killed God's servants, the prophets, and that they were also about to take the life of the Son of God.

The religious leaders were well aware that Jesus' parables were directed at them. For that reason they tried all the harder to find an occasion to arrest him and have him put away. They sent in questioners, who attempted to catch him in a contradiction or violation of the law. Their arsenal of questions included one that involved the hated duty of paying taxes to the Roman government: "Is it right to pay taxes to Caesar or not?" Jesus could not be taken in with such a question, however. His answer proved only to reveal his sincerity and insight. Calling attention to the image of Caesar on a Roman coin, Jesus advised the leaders to give to Caesar what was his due—and to God what was his. The more difficult their questions, the more amazed were the crowds at his answers. How simple he seemed to make it sound.

In some instances, such as the question the Sadducees leveled against Jesus regarding life in the resurrected state, even the teachers of the law themselves marveled at Jesus' answers. In the end his opponents were speechless and lost all nerve to ask further questions.

Jesus Turns the Table on His Opponents (Matt. 22:41–23:39; Mark 12:35–44; Luke 20:41–21:4; John 12:20–50)

When the questions of the religious leaders ceased, Jesus began to ask his own. What do the Old Testament Scriptures say about the Messiah, the Son of David? What was the meaning of specific messianic passages such as Psalm 110? As the crowd's attention turned to Jesus, they listened to him expound these texts. Jesus taught about simple godly virtues such as humility and graciousness and illustrated his points with human examples around him. Jesus showed how a poor widow who gave two small copper coins gave more than the petty gifts the rich bestowed on the house of God. Though the wealth of the rich had made the temple a beautiful sight to behold, its inward corruption and pride would soon result in its destruction.

Jesus' comments turned to rebuke. Like the prophet he was, he pronounced a series of seven woes against the leaders in Jerusalem (Matt. 23:1–39). The die was now cast.

In Jerusalem and at the temple at this time were many Greeks (Gentile converts to Judaism) who had come to celebrate the Feast of the Passover (John 12:20–28). Jesus saw them as a prelude to the great multitude of Gentile believers who would come to him after his death. As he spoke, a voice came from heaven that sounded like thunder. That voice, said Jesus, was a final confirmation that God had sent him and that the death he was about to endure was a fulfillment of his great purpose of redemption. As the prophets had foretold, many in the crowd did not believe. There were some, however, even among the religious leaders, who did believe. But they would not openly confess their faith because they were afraid that they might be put out of their synagogues by the Pharisees.

The End of the Ages
(Matt. 24:1–26:16; Mark 13:1–14:11;
Luke 21:5–22:6)

When he had finished speaking, Jesus left the temple for the last time. He made his way out of the city and to the Mount of Olives, where he taught his disciples what lay ahead for his people.

Having heard Jesus mention the destruction of the temple, the disciples asked when they could expect the "end of the age." Jesus then taught them about the last days—those days when the kingdoms of this world would be destroyed and his kingdom would be established.

After his discourse, Jesus warned his disciples of his own impending crucifixion. The Passover was to be celebrated in two days, and he would be handed over to the Romans to be crucified. At that precise moment the religious leaders were finalizing their plans to arrest Jesus. The chief priests and elders gathered at the palace of the high priest, Caiaphas, to hatch a plot that would eventually lead to the arrest and execution of Jesus. Their great fear was of inciting a riot during the Passover. They therefore acted with extreme caution.

Later that same night Judas Iscariot went to the chief priests and offered to reveal the whereabouts of Jesus. For this he was paid thirty silver coins. Having become a part of the conspiracy, Judas waited for the right opportunity to betray Jesus. It is generally believed that Jesus returned to Bethany that evening and remained there throughout the next day.

The Last Supper
(Matt. 26:17–29; Mark 14:12–25;
Luke 22:7–23; John 13:1–17:26)

While in Bethany, Jesus sent Peter and John to Jerusalem to prepare for the celebration of Passover. This was the first day of the Feast of Unleavened Bread, which was the day of the preparation of the Passover, Nisan 14 (April 6, A.D. 30). The disciples, following Jesus' instructions, found a large second-story room already prepared for a Passover celebration. There they made the final preparations.

When evening came and it was time to celebrate the Passover, Jesus was joined at the table by all twelve of his disciples. While they were eating, he began to speak about his betrayal. He openly acknowledged that one of the twelve disciples would betray him. As each denied any knowledge of a plot, Judas boldly asked, "Surely not I, Rabbi?" But Jesus replied, "Yes, it is you."

Jesus then served his disciples the bread and wine of the Passover meal. After Judas had taken the bread, he left the room. Those present who saw him leave thought he was going out to buy more food or to give money to the poor (John 13:27–30).

After the Passover, Jesus took the bread and cup and began to interpret them in light of the momentous events that were about to happen to him—his death on the cross. The bread he broke for them was his body, and the wine, his blood poured out for them. The Passover meal thus became a picture of the new covenant, which Jesus established with his death (Luke 22:20).

Before going out to be arrested and crucified, Jesus taught his disciples at length about his departure (John 13:31–16:33), after which he prayed a final prayer (John 17). Jesus and his disciples then sang a hymn and departed for the Mount of Olives.

Jesus in Gethsemane
(Matt. 26:30–46; Mark 14:26–42; Luke 22:24–46; John 18:1)

After the Passover, Jesus and his disciples walked through the city and crossed the Kidron Valley, east of Jerusalem, to the Mount of Olives. As they did so, a dispute broke out among them as to which of them was considered greatest. Jesus warned them that their attitude was entirely inconsistent with their mission. They had been called as servants, not as lords.

As they approached the secluded hillside, Jesus told his disciples that they would all fall away that night, just as the Old Testament prophets had foretold; but after his death, he would rise again and meet them in Galilee. Peter hastily vowed that he would never forsake Jesus, but Jesus warned him that he would, in fact, deny him three times before the early morning hour.

Earlier when Jesus had sent his disciples out to proclaim the coming of the kingdom of God, they were instructed to take no money for food or extra clothing. Now he commanded them to take money for food and clothing and a sword for protection.

Jesus and his disciples came to an orchard called Gethsemane on the Mount of Olives. This had been a favorite meeting place for them. Judas was also familiar with the site and knew Jesus would be there. Leaving his disciples behind, Jesus went to a secluded site with Peter, James, and John. He became sorrowful and troubled. Leaving the three disciples alone, he went off a short distance to pray. Though not wanting to undergo the suffering that lay ahead, he accepted it as God's will. After he finished praying, Jesus returned to his disciples only to find them sleeping. Disappointed that they had not kept vigil with him, he admonished them and continued to pray earnestly until the time drew near for his arrest. Jesus prayed so intently that the sweat dripped down from his forehead as if he were bleeding (Luke 22:44). An angel comforted him during this time (22:43).

Jesus' Arrest
(Matt. 26:47–56; 27:1–10; Mark 14:43–52; Luke 22:47–53; John 18:1–12)

When Jesus had finished praying, he returned to his disciples and awoke them. As they were speaking, a large detachment of heavily armed temple guards arrived, led by Judas. Some of the religious officials from Jerusalem also accompanied the guards. Judas greeted Jesus with a kiss, which was a prearranged signal to the guards. When they saw this, the guards moved in to take Jesus by force. Peter, quickly drawing his sword, attacked one of the guards and cut off his ear. Jesus rebuked Peter and healed the guard's ear. The temple guards then attempted to take Jesus by force, but they were unable to move. But Jesus offered no resistance. He accompanied them voluntarily, allowing himself to be bound and arrested.

When his disciples saw that Jesus had been arrested, they fled for their lives. Only a single young man continued to follow Jesus as the guards took him away. The guards, however, seized him, and in the struggle the young man escaped. The identity of that man is unknown.

Some time later, when Judas saw what was happening to Jesus, he deeply regretted what he had done. Having determined to make amends, he went into the meeting of the Sanhedrin to return the money that had been given him to betray Jesus. When the leaders refused to accept the money, Judas threw it on the floor of the temple and went away and hanged himself (cf. Acts 1:18–19). The temple officials, knowing where the money came from, were unwilling to put it into their treasury, so they used it to purchase a plot of land as a burial place for foreigners.

The Trial
(Matt. 26:57–68; Mark 14:53–65;
Luke 22:63–71; John 18:13–24)

Jesus was first taken to the house of Annas, the father-in-law of Caiaphas. He was then immediately taken to be examined by Caiaphas (John 18:24), where the entire Sanhedrin had already begun assembling for a trial. They had been preparing false evidence against Jesus. Two witnesses agreed to say they had heard Jesus speak of destroying the temple and rebuilding it in three days. Jesus, however, refused to speak in his own defense. The testimony of the two witnesses, in fact, proved to be contradictory, as did the other evidence presented at the trial.

When the testimony against Jesus began to fall apart, the high priest began to question Jesus about his disciples and his teaching—attempting to draw out some incriminating belief or teaching. Jesus responded by reminding him that he had taught openly in the temple and that there was nothing in his teaching that he had not already taught publicly. As Jesus was saying this, one of the officials looking on stepped forward and struck Jesus in the face.

In near desperation, the high priest commanded Jesus under oath to tell the Sanhedrin whether or not he was the divine Messiah. Jesus stated simply and without hesitation that he was. He then warned the high priest and the Sanhedrin that the glorious Old Testament prophecies about the establishment of the eternal kingdom of God were to be fulfilled in his second coming.

At this, the high priest charged Jesus with blasphemy and sentenced him to death. The Sanhedrin, not unexpectantly, concurred with this decision. Jesus was delivered to the guards, who mocked and beat him cruelly. Since it was late in the night, the final decision of the Sanhedrin was postponed until morning. Jesus remained under custody in the house of the high priest, where the guards continued to insult and torture him.

On the following morning, then, Jesus was brought before the Sanhedrin for further examination before sending him on to Pilate, the Roman governor. The Jewish officers continued to seek evidence of Jesus' messianic claims to present to the Roman officials. Jesus himself made no effort to deny his claim to be the Messiah. Having been assured of that, the officials took him to the governor, Pilate.

Peter's Denial
(Matt. 26:69–75; Mark 14:66–72;
Luke 22:54–62; John 18:15–18, 25–27)

The disciple John had followed Jesus to the house of the high priest, Caiaphas. Because he was known to the high priest, he was admitted into the house with the others. He waited in the courtyard, however. With John's help, Peter was also admitted into the courtyard.

While Jesus was being interrogated by Caiaphas, the servant girl who had admitted Peter into the courtyard recognized him as one of Jesus' disciples. When she asked Peter if he was, in fact, one of the disciples, he denied any association with Jesus. Peter had, by now, taken a place by the fire in the courtyard to warm himself. Those warming themselves around a fire by the gateway of the courtyard continued to ask him if he was one of Jesus' disciples. In response to their questions Peter denied Jesus two more times.

Just at the time of his third denial, a rooster began to crow—thus fulfilling Jesus' words to Peter that he would deny him three times "before the rooster crows" (John 13:38). In his present state of mind, Peter seems not to have noticed the significance of the rooster's crow. But during the events of the trial, when at one point Jesus caught his eye, Peter remembered what Jesus had said, left the courtyard, and "wept bitterly" (Luke 22:62).

Jesus Before Pilate and Herod
(Matt. 27:11-26; Mark 15:1-20; Luke 23:1-25)

Having determined to present their case against Jesus to the Roman authorities, the Sanhedrin turned Jesus over to the temple guards. They bound Jesus and led him off to Pilate. The religious leaders did not enter the Roman palace for fear of defiling themselves and hence being unable to celebrate Passover. Pilate thus came out to them and asked what charge they were bringing against Jesus. The leaders charged Jesus with many crimes, both religious and political. The leading charge was sedition: "We have found this man subverting our nation. He opposes payment of taxes to Caesar and claims to be Christ, a king" (Luke 23:2).

Hearing the charge against Jesus and finding little evidence to back it up, Pilate directed the leaders of the Sanhedrin to try Jesus in their own courts. They objected, however, since they had no authority to execute Jesus in their own law courts. Pilate therefore proceeded with the case by privately examining Jesus. He asked first whether Jesus did, in fact, claim to be the Jewish king, as he had been charged. By the nature of Jesus' response, Pilate concluded that Jesus was not a political threat and had not made any claims at grasping political power. He thus returned to the religious leaders and publicly declared Jesus to be innocent of their charges.

The leaders of the Sanhedrin, however, were not satisfied with this answer. They further charged Jesus with inciting sedition as far away as his homeland in Galilee. When Pilate heard that Jesus was from Galilee, he quickly rushed Jesus off to see Herod, the official to whom the Romans had given jurisdiction over Galilee.

Herod was pleased to see Jesus, having heard much about him, including the miracles he had performed. Herod asked Jesus many questions, but Jesus refused to answer them. The religious leaders continued their barrage of accusations against Jesus. Unable to come to a decision, Herod and his soldiers mocked Jesus by dressing him in a royal garment and sent him back to Pilate. Herod's tacit agreement with Pilate about the innocence of Jesus apparently pleased Pilate, since from that time on he looked favorably on his former enemy, Herod.

Bolstered by Herod's inability to convict Jesus, Pilate called together the religious leaders of Jerusalem and declared Jesus to be innocent. He had decided to set Jesus free. The crowd that had gathered around Pilate's palace, however, would not accept such a verdict. They chanted wildly, "Crucify him! Crucify him!" When Pilate offered to release Jesus as part of the Roman custom to release a popular prisoner at one of the feasts, the crowd chose the murderer Barabbas instead. There seemed to be no way to appease the fury of the crowd, which had been stirred up against Jesus by their religious leaders. Against his own wishes, Pilate was forced, in the end, to release Barabbas to them and turn Jesus over to his soldiers to be crucified.

In an act of final desperation, Pilate symbolically washed his hands before the crowd and declared his own innocence in sending Jesus off to be crucified. The crowds responded by willingly accepting the responsibility for Jesus' death.

The Crucifixion
(Matt. 27:27–56; Mark 15:16–41;
Luke 23:26–49; John 19:17–37)

In the courtyard of the palace, Pilate's soldiers mercilessly mocked Jesus before taking him out to be crucified. They stripped him of his clothes and dressed him as a king, placing a crown of thorns on his head and a staff in his hand. As they mocked him, the soldiers spat on him and hit him repeatedly with his staff. They then put his own clothes back on him and led him away, carrying his own cross.

As they walked to the place of execution called Golgotha (the Skull), the soldiers forced a man named Simon, from Cyrene in North Africa, to carry the cross for Jesus. As Jesus walked through the rest of the city, Simon followed him, along with a crowd of mourners. Jesus, however, quieted the mourners and warned that much more trauma lay ahead for the people of Jerusalem. When they arrived at Golgotha, they crucified Jesus. It was 9 A.M.

After nailing Jesus on the cross, they offered him a pain-killing drink of wine and gall flavored with myrrh, but Jesus refused. Jesus then prayed a prayer of forgiveness for those who had crucified him. Having stripped him of his clothing, the soldiers cast lots among themselves for them. A sign written in three languages (Aramaic, Latin, and Greek) was placed over his head on the cross. It read, "This is Jesus of Nazareth, the King of the Jews." The sign served, apparently, to notify the people about the main charge against Jesus. The religious leaders, however, protested to Pilate that the sign said too much. It should read, they argued, that Jesus "claimed" to be the king, not that he "was" the king. But Pilate let the sign stay as is.

On either side of Jesus the Romans crucified two robbers. One of them mocked Jesus as he died; the other reverently defended him. Jesus assured the latter that he would be with him in paradise. Bystanders hurled insults at Jesus, as did the chief priests and other religious leaders. From noon to 3 P.M., an ominous darkness covered the place where Jesus was crucified. Then Jesus cried out in his own native tongue the opening words of Psalm 22, "My God, my God, why have you forsaken me?" The crowd thought he was crying out to Elijah.

Jesus then cried out again, "I am thirsty." Someone nearby put a sponge filled with wine vinegar on a pole and offered it to Jesus to drink. Jesus then cried out, "Father, into your hands I commit my spirit," and with the words "It is finished" on his lips, he bowed his head and died.

The time of his death was in the late afternoon on the day of the Preparation of the Passover, at that same time as the Passover lambs were being slaughtered at the altar of the temple. When the soldiers came to finish off the three crucified men by breaking their legs and allowing them to suffocate, they found that Jesus had already died. Hence, they did not break his legs—just as it was forbidden to break the bones of the Passover lamb. One of the soldiers took his spear and thrust it into the side of Jesus' corpse; out flowed a mixture of blood and water.

At the moment of Jesus' death, the veil in the temple separating the Most Holy Place was torn from top to bottom. The earth shook and rocks split apart. Many tombs around the cities broke open, and dead people were raised up and later appeared throughout Jerusalem. A Roman centurion, looking on at all that happened, was heard to say, "Surely he was the Son of God."

Among the many present at Jesus' death were the women from Galilee who had traveled with Jesus and cared for him: Mary Magdalene, Mary the mother of James and Joses, and Salome the mother of Zebedee's sons. Mary the mother of Jesus, her sister, Mary the wife of Clopas, and the disciple John were also standing near the cross.

The Burial of Jesus
(Matt. 27:57–66; Mark 15:42–47;
Luke 23:50–56; John 19:38–42)

Since the death of Jesus occurred on the evening of a special feast day, the religious leaders would not permit his body to remain on the cross overnight. This custom was derived from the more general biblical mandate of not allowing the body of an executed criminal to remain exposed overnight (Deut. 21:22–23). A wealthy secret follower of Jesus, Joseph from the town of Arimathea in Judea, made a quick petition of Pilate for the burial rights of Jesus' body. Joseph was a member of the Sanhedrin, the body that had convicted Jesus, though he had not consented to their decision.

Having obtained permission, Joseph and Nicodemus, another prominent person in Jerusalem and a secret follower of Jesus, took the body of Jesus and prepared it for burial as Jewish custom dictated. They put the body in a nearby garden in a newly carved tomb, owned by Joseph. A large stone was placed at the entrance of the tomb.

Mary Magdalene and Mary the mother of Joses were sitting nearby watching the tomb. When they saw where Jesus was buried, they went home to prepare spices and perfumes for his body. They stayed at home the following day because it was the Sabbath of the Passover.

The day after Jesus was buried, the religious leaders, fearing that someone would steal the body of Jesus, requested that Pilate station a guard at the tomb. They remembered that Jesus had predicted his own resurrection on the third day, and they feared that his disciples would steal the body and make a claim that Jesus had risen from the dead. Pilate sent a detachment of guards to the tomb and sealed its entrance.

The Resurrection and Appearances of Jesus

The Resurrection of Jesus
(Matt. 28:1–10; Mark 16:1–8;
Luke 24:1–12; John 20:1–18)

On the day after the Passover Sabbath, on Sunday, the first day of the week, the two woman who had watched the burial of Jesus—Mary Magdalene and Mary the mother of Joses—returned to the tomb accompanied by Salome, Joanna, and others who had been with them at the crucifixion. They intended to anoint the body of Jesus with spices and perfumes, which they had prepared. Before they arrived at the tomb, however, an angel came to the tomb and shook the ground violently so that the stone at the entrance to the tomb was rolled away. The Roman guards were horrified and stunned, and they quickly fled the scene.

When the women arrived at the tomb, it was still dark, but Mary Magdalene could see that the stone had been removed from the entrance. Fearing that Jesus' body had been stolen, she immediately returned to tell Peter. Peter and John ran to the tomb at once and found it empty, just as the women had said. When they entered the tomb, they found the strips of linen and the burial cloth lying to one side. Peter and John returned to the city, but Mary and the other women remained at the tomb. As she sat weeping, Mary saw two angels, clothed in white, sitting in the tomb. One of the angels told the women that Jesus was no longer in the tomb because he had risen from the dead. They then told the women to return to the disciples and tell them that Jesus was already on his way to Galilee and that they would see him there.

As the women turned to leave and make their way back to the disciples in Jerusalem, they saw Jesus standing behind them. Mary, the first to speak, thought initially that he was one of the gardeners. When Jesus called her by name, however, she recognized him. The women bowed down to worship him. Jesus reiterated the message the angels had given the women. They were to tell the disciples to go to Galilee, where they themselves would see Jesus.

The Appearances of Jesus
(Matt. 28:11-20; Luke 24:13-49; John 20:19-21:23; Acts 1:3-8)

While the women were hurrying to the disciples, some of the guards who had been at the tomb when the angel rolled away the stone reported what they had seen to the chief priests. Hearing the report, the priests heavily rewarded the soldiers and told them to spread the word that Jesus' disciples had come during the night and stolen his body while they were asleep.

When the disciples heard the women's report of the resurrection of Jesus, they were at first skeptical. Peter returned to the tomb, but found it just as he had seen it earlier that morning. As he returned to Jerusalem, Peter was still puzzled at what he had seen and heard. That same day, two other followers of Jesus met him on their way to the small village of Emmaus. They did not, at first, recognize him. Later as they sat to eat together in Emmaus, they saw that it was Jesus who had accompanied them along the way. They returned to tell the disciples in Jerusalem they had been with Jesus. When they arrived, they found that Jesus had already appeared to Peter (cf. 1 Cor. 15:5), so they each related their stories of seeing Jesus.

As they were speaking, Jesus came and stood in their midst and greeted them. At first the disciples were startled and thought he was a ghost. Then Jesus calmed them and showed them his hands and feet, and he ate a meal with them.

One of the disciples, Thomas, was not with them in the room. When he returned, the others told him they had seen Jesus. Thomas, however, vowed not to believe their report—at least not until he saw with his own eyes the Jesus he had seen crucified. A week later, when the disciples were together again in the same room, Jesus came and stood in their midst. Thomas was with them this time. When he saw Jesus, he also believed. The disciples then went to Galilee, where they found Jesus. Even then, some among the disciples doubted what they had seen.

Jesus was with his disciples for a period of forty days. During this time he continued to work miracles and to teach them about the coming kingdom of God. On one occasion when the disciples had fished all night in the Sea of Galilee and had caught no fish, Jesus came to them in the early morning along the shore and told them to cast their nets on the right side of the boat. When they did, they caught a large haul of fish and were unable to bring them into the boat. Peter realized that it could only be Jesus who had called out to them, and he jumped into the water and waded to shore. When they had pulled their nets ashore, they found they had a catch of 153 large fish. Jesus already had a fire waiting on the shore, and with it they prepared some of their catch for breakfast. Jesus took that occasion to remind Peter and the disciples of the importance of feeding the growing band of young believers who had begun to follow Jesus.

Jesus gave a final word of instruction to his disciples, commanding them to spread the news of his resurrection and teaching throughout the world. He also commanded them to remain in Jerusalem until the coming of the Holy Spirit. After that they were to go throughout Judea and Samaria and throughout the world as witnesses to Jesus the Messiah.

The Ascension (Luke 24:50–53; Acts 1:9–11)

At the end of the forty days in which Jesus remained with his disciples, he brought them to Bethany and began to bless them. While he was blessing them, Jesus was taken up into heaven, disappearing finally behind a cloud. As they watched the heavens where he had ascended, two angels dressed in white appeared beside them and told them that Jesus would return in the future, just as he had left.

The disciples and those with them returned to Jerusalem and continued to worship God at the temple.

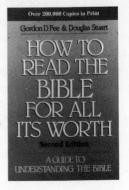
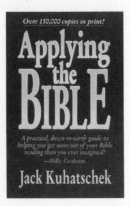

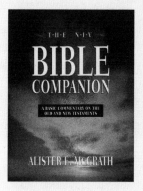

More books by John Sailhamer

The NIV Compact Series

This four-volume series sits handsomely on your desk or bookshelf, ready to answer your Bible study questions quickly and authoritatively. If you read the NIV Bible, then you need this series.

NIV Compact Concordance, by John R. Kohlenberger III and Edward W. Goodrick
   0-310-59480-4

NIV Compact Bible Commentary, by John Sailhamer
   0-310-51460-6

NIV Compact Nave's Topical Bible, by John R. Kohlenberger III
0-310-40210-7

NIV Compact Dictionary of the Bible, by J. D. Douglas and Merrill C. Tenney
0-310-33180-3

The Pentateuch as Narrative
A Biblical-Theological Commentary

Understand the first five books of the Bible as their author originally intended. Dr. Sailhamer presents the Pentateuch as a coherent whole, revealing historical and literary themes that appear clearly only when it is read this way. A fresh look at the beginnings of the nation of Israel and the earliest foundations of the Christian faith.

Softcover: 0-310-57421-8

Available at your local Christian bookstore.

ZondervanPublishingHouse
Grand Rapids, Michigan

A Division of HarperCollins*Publishers*

http://www.zondervan.com